Violetta Thurstan -- a celebration

Violetta Thurstan -- a celebration

by Muriel Somerfield and Ann Bellingham

with a foreword by Mary Barker

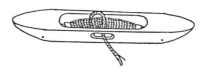

Jamieson Library
Newmill, Penzance, Cornwall
1993

First published in Great Britain in 1993 for the Jamieson Library of Women's History by the Patten Press (Publishers). The Old Post Office, Newmill, Penzance, Cornwall TR20 4XN.

ISBN 1 872229 08 5

Typesetting & graphic illustration in-house at The Patten Press. Photographic work by David Scholes.
Printed and bound in Great Britain by The Cromwell Press, Broughton Gifford, Melksham, Wiltshire

Table of contents

List of illustrations

Foreword

Her friends will welcome this monograph about Violetta Thurstan and her adventurous, exciting life. The two authors have chosen well in linking it to the 40th anniversary of the Cornwall Guild of Weavers, Spinners and Dyers as Violetta was their beloved President for many years. Violetta Thurstan was - and indeed still is - well known to weavers both here and overseas through her books, *The Use of Vegetable Dyes for Beginners* and *A Short History of Ancient and Decorative Textiles*, but few realise the part she played in the two world wars.

When Violetta came up to London to visit exhibitions we often met and on all these occasions she gave me advice and encouragement, as indeed she did always to weavers, spinners and dyers. Her frail appearance gave no hint of her immense determination and lively spirit. May this monograph lead many others to share in my admiration for the many achievements of this very distinguished lady, Violet Anna Thurstan.

Mary Barker, M.B.E.

Introduction

When the Cornwall Guild of Weavers, Spinners and Dyers was planning their 40th Anniversary in 1992, the name of Violetta Thurstan kept appearing in old scrap books. Articles hinted at a life far beyond the confines of Cornwall and the world of textiles. Melissa Hardie at the Jamieson Library of Women's History, Newmill, suggested that here was a woman who deserved further investigation.

This work was originally dependent on sources found up to October 1992, but a visit to Magdalene College, Cambridge, in May 1993 revealed a hitherto unknown set of 16 diaries written by Violetta. Collating this further information meant a complete re-write of the manuscript in hand, and this proved both exciting and frustrating. The end result remains a jigsaw with many missing pieces. We hope by highlighting certain points in Violetta's life, others will be inspired to research in greater depth.

Many remember her with affection, respect, and in some cases, awe. Using the information shared so generously, we have attempted to present a sequence of events in a factual and objective way. For ease of reading, two conventions have been employed in the text of this monograph. Violetta's own words from her diary entries are presented throughout in italic type, whereas small print is used to indicate longer extracts, letters, speeches by both Violetta and others corresponding subsequently with the authors about her. All the research information, letters, tapes and notes relating to this publication are held by the Jamieson Library, Newmill, Penzance, Cornwall, and are available for perusal.

MMS
AVB
Jamieson Library 1993

Chapter 1

What's in a name

Anna Violet Thurstan deliberately altered her name and chose to be known throughout her working life, corre-spondence, and to her friends as Violetta. To her immediate family she was 'Vi'. In an anecdote recalled by a friend of Violetta this name change was 'a mere affectation of hers.'[1] She claimed her forebears to be 'proud Cornish seafarers living near St. Columb'. 'I was just born in England,' Viol-etta reflected 'and then the family went to live in the Canaries'.[2]

Violetta came from a comfortable, well-educated and much travelled family, which must have encouraged her to continue studying and learning throughout her long life. Born on 4 February, 1879 in Hastings, Sussex, in later life she celebrated her birthday on February 2nd, Candlemass day and a festival of purification of our Lady for Roman Catholics, the faith which Violetta adopted. She regularly altered the year of her birth according to her applications for changes of service in a variety of different fields of work.

The Foreign and Commonwealth Office knew her birth as 4 February 1891.[3] The obituary in *The Times* on Monday, 17th April 1978, recorded that she died aged 97, but her family and records show that she was 99. Her burial was in the Roman Catholic section of the Falmouth Lawn Cemetery, Cornwall, on 19th April 1978.

Her fragile, slightly untidy, appearance in photographs and in person, hid a remarkably strong will. Violetta held definite views about most things and is remembered as someone who, while compassionate in nature, nevertheless liked always to be in charge. She coped stoically with hardships and illness, and shared many qualities with other well-known travellers who had preceded her. Gertrude Bell, who also travelled extensively in the Middle East and spoke several languages like Violetta, was the subject of a much cherished birthday gift which Violetta received in 1929, *Letters of Gertrude Bell*.[4] Violetta herself listed that she 'knew French and German well, Spanish and Italian, enough Russian and Swedish to get on, used to have Arabic but now forgotten'.[5] Lady Anne Blunt was cool and level-headed like Violetta and she too knew the Bedouins of Egypt, writing her adventures in the year of Violetta's birth. But, unlike these more famous individuals, the total kaleidoscope of Violetta's achievements have gone largely unrecognised.

Violetta was a restless person. Throughout life she strove to educate and encourage others to develop their talents, travel abroad and be of service. Assiduously she followed up contacts with influential personages so as to maximise opportunities that would help her in difficult situations. Yet her achievements, though individual, are not unprecedented when placed alongside those of others in her time.

Many Victorian and Edwardian women wrote informative or instructive articles, moral tales and short stories which appeared in journals like *Harper's Magazine*, *Sunday at Home*, *The Strand* and *The Temple*. There is a wealth and depth of writing by women aimed at middle-class house-

2

holds from 1875 to 1925, and the imperialist brashness of the empire provided readers with exciting tales of daring and adventure.

Violetta wrote avidly and published records of her exploits in a range of books, letters and articles. These were interlaced with learned writings about weaving, one of which in its 17th edition is still regarded today as being definitive for students. Latterly, she arranged for the private printing of three novels.

****

Little is known about Violetta's relationships with her parents. It is understood that her father was Cornish [6], while her mother is believed to have been Scottish. [7] Violetta gave her childhood home in various records as being alternatively in Cornwall or in the Canary Isles. The University of St. Andrews, with which she had an external study link in her twenties, lists her birthplace as Egypt. [8] In the *Tenerife News,* there is mention of an E. Paget Thurstan, M.D., Cant. and Mrs. Thurstan and family having lived there in 1888. [9]

The house where the Thurstan family resided in the Santa Catalina region of the Canaries, is no longer there. [10] This is a particular disappointment since the heroine of Violetta's later novel, *Stormy Petrel,* is placed as living there at Casa Marina. Violetta wrote 'the first thing I can remember was Casa Marina - the most beautiful place in the world, we thought.' [11] *Stormy Petrel* was written in 1964 when she was 85, and other vivid descriptions within it mirror incidents in her childhood, which make it possible to regard the novel as having autobiographical aspects, though stated as being 'wholly fictional'.

Charles Thurstan, Violetta's nephew, commented that her parents were constantly on the move, but spent some holidays in the Canaries and also in Paignton, Devon. He thought the family lived in Bath and possibly Jersey. In one

3

diary Violetta refers to a visit to Nanswydyn and held this to be the ancestral home in Cornwall. It seems, however, that for the whole of their lives together the family nomadically moved from job to job, country to country. At one point, Violetta's father went briefly to Australia [12] while the boys and their mother returned to Torquay. Violetta was sent to school in Germany. This is consistently mentioned in international directories of distinguished people printed and reprinted throughout the years of her life. However disruptive this might have been, all four children remained close, and jointly inherited a love of travel.

From Violetta's writings it is clear that she continued a regular, although casual, contact with her father and 'Aunt Louise' (his sister) after she entered her adult years. When the three coincided in a visit to England they stayed with each other for the occasional night. No references to her maternal family have been found, and even the date of her mother's death is unknown.

Violetta was especially fond of her elder brother, Edward Paget Thurstan, C.M.G. *and his wife, Christina. Padge, as he was called, had an outstanding career in the Foreign Office, serving in Europe, America, Africa and South Africa. Vi stayed with Padge and Tina at least once a year, obviously enjoying the social life at the various European postings. Bridge, sherry, tea and tennis parties are the recorded activities peppering Violetta's diaries along with lively comments on both the places and circumstances. Her sisterly concern is noted in her diaries and correspondence when either are ill. Two bleak references refer to '16 February 1944, Tina died' and '3 April 1947 Heard today about P. Died evening of operation.' Her brother had died on the 26th March, but because Violetta was still working in Austria with post-war relocation services, it had taken eight

*Companion of St. Michael & St. George.

days to get the news to her. Christina and Paget's son, John Denzil Boyd Paget Thurstan (called JP) proved to be a loving nephew and companion to Violetta for the rest of her life.

Her second brother, Norman, R.N., D.S.O.[13], after a distinguished service career in the Far East and Europe, raced *The Julie Breeze* in the Fastnet Race, before retiring to Paignton, Devon. This was the home that Violetta often visited. Norman's elder son, Charles, and wife, Margaret, now retired in England, have been a major source of information for this monograph. Their second son, Richard, died in 1947. Little information is known about Violetta's youngest brother, Denzil. He served with honour in the Navy but died in 1919.

p. 5 Thurstan family portrait. Violetta with Denzil (L), Edward and Norman.

5

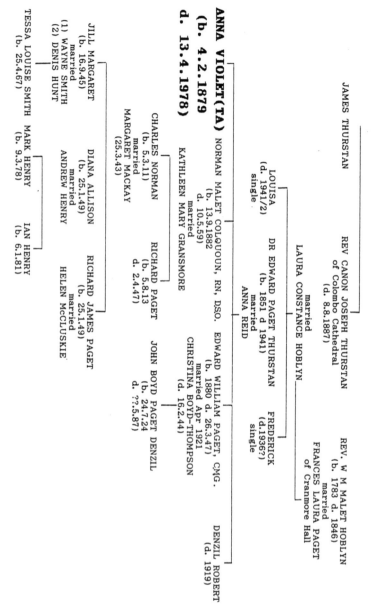

JAMES THURSTAN

REV CANON JOSEPH THURSTAN of Colombo Cathedral (d. 8.8.1887)
married
LAURA CONSTANCE HOBLYN

REV. W M MALET HOBLYN (b. 1783 d. 1846)
married
FRANCES LAURA PAGET of Cranmore Hall

ANNA VIOLET(TA)
(b. 4.2.1879
d. 13.4.1978)

LOUISA (d. 1941/2) single

DR EDWARD PAGET THURSTAN (b. 1851 d 1941)
married
ANNA REID

FREDERICK (d.1936?) single

NORMAN MALET COLQUOUN, RN, DSO. (b. 13.9.1882 d. 10.5.59)
married
KATHLEEN MARY GRANSMORE

EDWARD WILLIAM PAGET, CMG. (b. 1880 d. 26.3.47)
married Apr 1921
CHRISTINA BOYD-THOMPSON (d. 16.2.44)

DENZIL, ROBERT (d. 1919)

CHARLES NORMAN (b. 5.3.11)
married
MARGARET MACKAY (25.3.43)

RICHARD PAGET (b. 5.8.13 d. 2.4.47)

JOHN BOYD PAGET DENZIL (b. 24.7.24 d. ??.5.87)

JILL MARGARET (b. 16.9.45)
married
(1) WAYNE SMITH
(2) DENIS HUNT

DIANA ALLISON (b. 25.1.49)
married
ANDREW HENRY

RICHARD JAMES PAGET (b. 25.1.49)
married
HELEN McCLUSKIE

TESSA LOUISE SMITH (b. 25.4.67)

MARK HENRY (b. 9.3.78)

IAN HENRY (b. 6.1.81)

Researched and presented by
Charles and Margaret Thurstan (1992)

Further References to the Hoblyn & Vyvyan connections can be traced in
Vol 1 MacClaus Trigg Minor & Gentlemens Magazine
LXX/123 held at the Morrab Library, Penzance

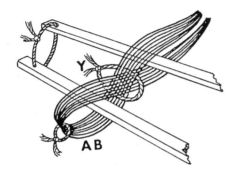

AB

Chapter 2

Education

The formal education of Violetta Thurstan is almost as complex to puzzle out as the conflicting information provided about her birth. She told a friend that she was 'dumped in a very strict German school which she hated. Her parents thought she needed discipline and a good, strong hand because she had been riding and running wild.' [1] Another source [2] has her educated in France, Germany, the Ladies College, Guernsey, as well as being tutored privately. While she may have been unhappy during these youthful studies, they undoubtedly served her well in giving her early practice with languages.

What is clear is that Violetta from time to time deliberately embroidered or eliminated details concerning her childhood. Apart from presumptions that may come from interpreting her novel *Stormy Petrel*, there is no definitive information about her formative years.

The first independent confirmation of Violetta's preparation for her future life, appears in 1898, when at the age of 19, she worked at the Home for Incurables in Wibney (sic). After one year, she moved to the East London Hospital for Children, and twelve months later she was working at the Fever Hospital in Guernsey. [3] Within a two year period, then, she had apprenticed herself to nursing. She was living at Apple Tree Cottage, Kingston, Taunton, Somerset, at the end of that two year preparation, when she furthered her plans by applying to train as a nurse at the London Hospital, Whitechapel. On the 29th December 1900 she arrived there as a probationer. This was the hospital where five years earlier Edith Cavell enrolled. [4]

The Matron of the London Hospital at that time was the outstanding Eva Charlotte Luckes who had a powerful influence on all who met her. A friend of Florence Nightingale, she was an innovative nurse educator, and doughty fighter for improved conditions for her nurses and their patients. Hospitals at the end of the 19th century were often housed in dark, miserable buildings, poorly equipped and funded. Some were regarded as charitable establishments fit only for the poor, with the better-off Victorians choosing to be treated and nursed at home. Miss Luckes' nurses had excellent training both for institutional care and in patients' homes, her 'Visiting Nurses' were second to none, and therefore demand exceeded the women available to take up these posts.

Violetta took up residence at Tredegar House, Bow, one of the preliminary training homes for nurses established by Miss Luckes. Each nurse had her own room and after passing a fitness examination each probationer undertook a six week preliminary training course, another of Miss Luckes' ideas. The probationers worked in groups of 20 away from the wards and learned to bandage, make beds, and other simple ward tasks while attending lectures on anatomy, hygiene and physiology. A pupil could then withdraw after taking the examination if she or the Hospital felt nursing was not suitable for her.

8

Successful candidates proceeded to the wards and, when they had completed their two years of training, became staff nurses or joined the private nursing staff for a further two years under contract. The salary varied from 24-45 pounds a year. In the period from 1880 to 1905 the London Hospital trained 1,200 nurses for Britain and the world. Violetta gained an honorary certificate in nursing on 11 March 1905. Her work was described as 'satisfactory', examination 'satisfactory', conduct 'very good' and sick room cookery 'excellent'. [5]

Violetta began work on the Sophia Ward and, despite intermittent spells of illness herself, gained a wide range of experience, covering as Assistant Holiday Sister in the Jewish Rothschild Ward, the Royal Ward and the Millward Ward. In 1903 she was back at Tredegar House, then in January 1904 off to Buxton before being posted as sister in charge of a small convalescent unit at Hythe, Kent. The latter was a home supported by the Eversley School for patients of the London Hospital. [6]

Red Cross records show that Violetta listed her previous work as a 'Home Sister, then a Matron at the Newcastle Hospital, a County Superintendent ending up as Matron at the Spezzia Hospital.' The Archive Section of the Red Cross can only place this latter posting as being on the Greek Island of Spetsia. [7]

Certainly this was an exciting time for those involved in medicine and nursing. Advances were bringing remarkable changes to patient care and treatment. In the 20 years leading up to 1905 malaria had been identified, X-rays discovered and the nature of adrenalin understood. Aspirin was introduced and Pasteur successfully inoculated a child bitten by a dog infected with rabies. Marie Stopes, the youngest Doctor of Science at 24, was formulating her policy on sex and birth control.

Violetta, never still for long, returned to England in 1907 having decided to pursue a different course of studies, which in 1914, resulted in her award of the 'Lady Literate

9

in Arts Diploma (LLA)' by the University of St. Andrews. [8] This was an external diploma awarded to women which could be taken at various examination centres around the world. In 1907 she began studying, giving her address as The Royal Infirmary, Bristol, where she took French and Geography both to pass level through the Tutorial Correspondence College, Colchester. In the following year she sat at the Devonport examination centre and took French to honours standard. In 1910 she succeeded in taking Geography to honours standard at the London examination centre and obtained a pass grade in Fine Art. At that stage she listed her education as being undertaken privately, indicating that she was pursuing her studies under her own impetus. In 1911 at the Leeds examination centre she passed English to Honours Standard C before returning to the London centre in 1913 to pass English Honours B. Her education then was recorded as through a 'Tutorial Institute' which presumably describes a correspondence course.

Back at the Bristol centre in 1914, she took physiology to pass standard, listing her education as private, and at that stage she had completed the course and was awarded the LLA Diploma. Later Violetta refers to all of these studies as 'Honours in Modern Languages, St. Andrews University.' Robert Smart [9] of St. Andrews University, commented that 'This record gives an impression of a very restless but persistent individual', characteristics which Violetta was to display throughout her life. One acquaintance of Violetta's during their Plymouth days,'was astonished to learn that she too was a graduate of my own University, and even more amazed to learn that Violetta had such a varied and distinguished career'. [10]

10

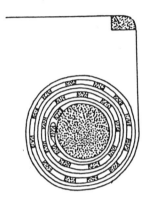

Chapter 3

War, War, War

In June 1914 the Archduke Ferdinand and his morga-
natic wife Sophie visited Bosnia, and on June 28th were shot
dead in Sarajevo by Gavrilo Princip, an assassin member of
the Serbian Black Hand. [1] Austria attacked Serbia, and
Germany, ruled by Kaiser Wilhem II, joined them in declaring war on Russia and then on France. Germany invaded
Belgium, Britain declared war on Austria and Germany.
Japan declared war on Germany.

The First World War was underway, and Violetta was
then 35 years old.

*War, war, war. For me the beginning of the War was a
torchlight tattoo on Salisbury plain. It was held on one of those
breathless evenings in July when the peace of Europe was
trembling in the balance and most of us had a heartache in case
England, at this time of internal crisis did not rise to the supreme
sacrifice.*

With the paragraph above, Violetta opens her book
Field Hospital and Flying Column, published in 1915 while

she was recovering from illness in England.[2] Later she would write *Hounds of War Unleashed, A Nurse's Account of her life on the Eastern front during the 1914-18 War.* [3] In that later account she described the start of the war for her in a more detailed way.

The Rally was held in a field which slanted steeply to a sea white with heat. In the far corner, the horses were nibbling delicately at the short thyme-covered turf; overhead the gulls were swooping and wheeling, watching intently to see if there were any bits and pieces left from our picnic lunch. We FANYS (First Aid Nursing Yeomanry). were lolling on the grass, wishing we could bathe. Our Training officer came along then: "If you young things haven't signed yet, you had better go along to the Commandant's tent and do it now."

Three or four of us jumped up. "What are we signing for?" I asked.

"You sign that you are willing to serve if there is ever a war. I think it is only a formality."

We presented ourselves and it was only a formality. We returned to our training class. The Training Manual said that wounded men should be wrapped warmly in blankets to lessen shock.

I remembered that, much later, when there were no blankets.

Violetta had joined the No. 46 Westminster Detachment of the British Red Cross Society in 1913 and, on the 4th August 1914, she was called up for service, told to report to the Red Cross Centre in Vincent Square. First, she helped some Voluntary Aid Detachment members (VADs) to improvise a temporary hospital at Faversham. Following this she was asked by the St. John Ambulance to take a party of nurses to Brussels to work under the authority of the Belgian Red Cross Society.

It was a time of great confusion, and eventually with only one nurse accompanying her, she left Charing Cross Station for Oostende. The Germans had declared Belgium neutral so as to establish a route through to France, and according to Violetta, Brussels seemed to be 'en fete - flags waving - everyone wearing badges or ribbons intertwined with British and Belgian colours.'(4) Nevertheless the threat of invasion was ever-present and Violetta attempted to stop the group of other nurses leaving England. Later she learned that her telegram had never been sent and that 26 nurses instead of the original 16 planning to come, were already on their way. In fact they arrived on the last train at the *Gare du Nord* before the Germans broke their agreement and entered Belgium as conquerors. Refugees were crowding into Brussels and all the Red Cross and medical service throughout Belgium were mobilised to help the wounded. Altogether, 1500 beds were set up in the city.

Though Violetta was a shrewd administrator it took her quite a while to disperse the nurses. 'How should I have borne it, I wondered, if it had been London. The streets were crowded but there was hardly a sound and the Germans took possession of Brussels in silence.' Many of the German soldiers were utterly exhausted. It took 36 hours before the final Red Cross wagons arrived. The city had fallen and they were cut off.

Violetta, initially, was helping to improvise a 130 bed hospital at a fire station in Brussels. Ten days later the Burgomaster of Charleroi requested nursing help and three volunteers came forward, Violetta and two Catholic Sisters, Elsie and Grace. Ten minutes later they were on their way. Charleroi was burning and the devastation was almost total. The French, Belgian and German wounded had very little food and conditions were generally desperate. All windows had to be shut in case anyone 'should fire on the Germans.'

Installed as Matron at Marcelline, the Germans gave Violetta authority to undertake any improvements she felt necessary. Supplies were difficult and the wounded kept on arriving. Nonetheless she remembered this as a 'very happy time.' There was no contact with England and she worried about her two younger brothers who were both serving in the Navy. All information came from enemy propaganda and the news was never good. However, she recognised the efficient organisational qualities of the Germans, even noting that the captured Pickford vans and Lyons Tea wagons were immediately painted the standard German grey before being put out to service.

On September 1st, the German Commander arrived at 7 a.m. to inform the staff of the immediate evacuation of the German wounded. Many would not stand the journey but despite protestations, all were removed. Violetta was then told that the French patients were to be transferred to prisons in Germany and again the Committee, led by Violetta, pleaded for the worst cases to stay. All left, only to return hours later to their disinfected beds from the station. Less than 24 hours later they were dispatched again.

With few Belgian patients left, she obtained a two day pass to Brussels to visit her nurses. On the way to locate one colleague serving in Tirlemout, an outlying village, Violetta and a companion nurse got lost, stumbling up to the German front line. They were sent to Brussels after a night in a French convent. This one incident highlights the isolation and terrifying circumstances which these devoted nurses encountered while serving abroad. Once in Brussels, Violetta was refused permission to return to Marcelline. The Germans shut down all the private ambulances and hospitals and no wounded were allowed to be nursed by Red Cross staff, who were now regarded as spies. On October 1st Brussels was formally declared German territory. Violetta, inoculated against typhoid suffered a severe reaction, so that when she was due to be evacuated through an American humanitarian plan, she was unable to travel.

The next day, all the English nurses and doctors serving in Belgium were ordered to leave. There was one exception. Edith Cavell, having trained and worked at the London Hospital during some shared periods with Violetta, was allowed to remain with her nurses. These had worked in

Belgium since 1910, establishing nurse training methods at St. Gilles. All the rest of the personnel were taken by train into Germany, passing through Munster and Hamburg, and being subjected to constant insults. None realised that they were to be exchanged at Vendrup on the Danish border, so the levels of anxiety were high throughout the trip. When they crossed the Kiel Canal, Violetta wrote *'after two months of being prisoners with no news of home - it was wonderful to see friendly, smiling faces.'* (5)

During her period of recovery in Denmark Violetta learned that her brothers were safe. At one point she met Madam Tscherning, President of the Danish Council of Nurses, and known as the 'Florence Nightingale of Denmark' She also met Prince Gustav and agreed that he should ask for her transfer with three other nursing sisters to serve with the Russian Red Cross. This request was made through his mother, the Dowager Russian Empress, Marie Federova. Violetta describes the latter as being 'Royal to her fingertips, racy, forceful, amusing, she was something more. I talked to her quite freely.'(6) It was explained that Prince and Princess Volkonsky had a First Aid Ambulance Unit at the front with General Ivanov's Third Army, and Violetta offered to serve there.

The nurses were attached to the Community of Sisters at Smolny and undertook 'instructions in Russian and their methods of First Aid.' The Smolny Convent was later used by Lenin in 1917 as his headquarters, and subsequently became the symbol of the October Revolution. The ballrooms were filled with wounded and the royal princesses, Anastasia, Maria and Tatiana came in to help. On one occasion the patients were visited by the Tsarina.

Soon she learned they were to leave for Warsaw to join the Flying Field Ambulance Surgery Service led by the Prince and Princess Volkonsky. There would be three sisters and an English surgeon with support staff, and this would be one of a number of mobile Ambulance Services run by the Russians. Another much larger ambulance unit (four surgical sisters, five nurses, 30 orderlies and a stores & catering officer, with 24 horse-drawn canvas wagons to bring in the wounded) operating at the same time, was staffed by Florence Farmborough, a 26 year old governess in Moscow who had immediately trained with the Red Cross at the outbreak of the war. Florence served in horrendous circumstances continuously up to 1918 when she was forced to flee the country on the Trans-Siberian Express. Her diary of over 400,000 words, now edited as *Nurse at the Russian Front*, offers graphic descriptions of the terrors of those days. (7) Like Violetta she too was awarded the Russian George Cross.

Violetta left Smolny for Warsaw. It proved a terrifying four day journey. The big battle was at Lodz and she arrived to find the hospital overwhelmed with wounded soldiers. *'We worked day and night. The hospital was dirty, the patients lay on straw and the food was poor but through it all the devotion was incredible as was the contact between officers and men.'* The unit had five ambulances and Violetta was in charge of surgical supplies, with *'one basin and one towel for 70 wounded. The shops were open but empty, and civilians slunk along the streets looking shabby and cold.'*

The Germans were advancing. It was bitterly cold and the nurses did not dare to wash the patients. The Unit was ordered to withdraw from Lodz back to Warsaw where they were greeted by Grand Duchess Anastasia. Violetta, now seriously unwell, suffered a shrapnel injury from a bomb dropped by a German plane. She caught a chill that turned to pleurisy and on 5th March 1915 she was sent back to England.

We can only speculate what her thoughts might have been when she heard of the proclamation some six months later on October 12, posted in Brussels, announcing the death of 27 people who had committed 'heinous crimes'. One of these was Edith Cavell.

Back in England she worked with the National Union of Trained Nurses, and her second book about the war, *The*

People Who Run, was published. [8] This stark, devastatingly critical, assessment of the dilemma of rootless refugees expelled in 1915, sadly mirrors the 'ethnic cleansing' of our present 1990s. Her persuasive argument is her declaration that 'the greatest tragedy of war is not seen on the battle field - it is the "people who run".' There could be no more appropriate title for those five and a half million dazed and terrified people who fled from their homes in the summer and autumn of 1915 before the German advance into Russia.

From the farms and homesteads of Poland, the peaceful plains of Lithuania, the seaports of the Baltic provinces, from the mountains of Galicia and Ruthenia they fled, to escape the roaring cannon and the devastating fire of the enemy. [9]

Their new home, the interior of Russia, was to them a foreign country where the language, religion and customs differed very much from their own; but their exile was made as little painful as possible by the kindness of the Russian peasants...The sympathy and compassion were there; alas, that there was no organisation ready also to cope with the awful need!

Violetta returned to Russia in 1916 to distribute funds and help to organise the English Hospital Units set up to help the thousands of refugees that had fled before the German invasions. On the 4th November 1916 she was sent to be matron of the 1000 bed hospital at La Panne in Belgium, the *Hopital de L'Ocean* where she remained for nine months. The evidence of her achievements and the affection in which she was held is seen through comments made by colleagues in a small autograph book now held by Magdalene College, Cambridge. This simple but moving tribute was presented to her when she left to begin work with Miss Murren at the Y Corps, Main Dressing Station, in France on 24th July 1917.

Less than two months later, suffering from shell shock, she was again sent home where she was informed that she had been awarded the Military Medal, one of only twenty

17

women to be so honoured. [10] Two months later, on 6th December 1917, she was well enough to travel to Macedonia and joined Dr. Bennett's Unit as Matron at Ostrovo. There she remained until on 30th June 1918 she returned to Taunton in Somerset. It would only be a bare two weeks later that she would hear of the summary execution of the Russian royal family at Ekaterinburg on 16th July. Later when questioned about Rasputin, and asked if she had met him, she replied that she had but 'she had not liked him because he had such a floppy handshake.' [11]

p. 18 Violetta on the occasion of receiving The Military Medal.

Chapter 4

Beginning to weave

After the war, Violetta, now in her late thirties, went to Sweden for six months to train in 'weaving and handicrafts' at the August Abrahamson College at Maff near Goteberg. Later, Violetta listed her achievements there as 'Weaving and Textile Design, August Abrahamson College, Sweden with three Diploma d'onore from Italy, Paris and Berlin together with two Swedish diplomas for textile work.'[1]

Sweden had a fine reputation as a centre for hand weaving. Violetta had travelled through Sweden en route to Russia previously in 1915, and contacts may well have been made then. She shared knowledge of this country with her brother Denzil, who in 1912, went from Stockholm to Finland en route to St. Petersburg and Moscow. [2]

References to her Swedish training are made briefly in the acknowledgements of her book *Weaving Without Tears*, which was published in 1956.[3] In it, she comments on new methods and materials and admits that 'methods that one

19

thought immutable as the stars in one's student days in Sweden are superseded.' This would appear to be the only formal training in weaving that Violetta received. Her next adventure began in the early 1920s when she was appointed as Director of the Bedouin Industries for the Egyptian Government. Her post was under the auspices of the War Office and had some connection with Lord Allenby. The Industries themselves were located in the Libyan Desert west of Cairo.

Prior to reading the evidence in her diaries, this would seem to have been a solitary and unique experience for a single woman in her forties. It is documented by Violetta in her memorable article in the *Quarterly Journal of Weavers, Spinners and Dyers* in March, 1959, written when she was 80 years old. It is reprinted in its entirety in Appendix I. For further reference to concise descriptions of weaving methods employed, see Violetta's book *A Short History of Decorative Textiles.* [4]

Many anecdotes from other articles, and from those who knew Violetta, come from this period in Egypt. A macabre story, told by her and recalled by a member of the Cornwall Guild tells of an Arab, one of the Bedouin workforce, who went missing for six weeks. Eventually he was found at the bottom of the well from which they were drawing their drinking water! [5]

In 1966 Violetta lectured to the London Guild of Weavers. [6] She elaborated on her Bedouin Industries' experiences, giving specific numbers of her workforce: a total of seven hundred people, two hundred spinners, three hundred weavers, the rest packers and helpers.

One reference in the report on the same 1966 lecture, was about five year old boys collecting reeds which the old men made into weaving reeds with wood at the top and bottom. In her original account Violetta says, when explaining how tents are woven, that 'there is no reed; the strands of wool are too close and thick for that'. She then goes on, 'carpets and rugs are made by the same method'.

20

There is no mention of fabrics that would be woven using a reed.

On one occasion a particular carpet was being woven for a king. This required an exceptionally long warp of 30 yards and in this instance a woman weaver sat on the warp to keep the tension and moved further and further up as the work progressed 'until she was nearly out of sight'. An explicit photograph of a Borg el Arab woman weaving in this way is included with a comprehensive chapter on Bedouin rugs in *Egyptian Carpets*, by Luanne Brown and Sidna Rachid.[7] It shows the woman sitting on the woven cloth with the leashes through which the warp is threaded suspended on a thick stick which is supported on tin cans. Violetta gave a Borg or Burg rug to Peter Collingwood, [8] woven in neutrals with a stripe of indigo.

The number of years Violetta was in Egypt and employed at the Industries is not clear. The earliest diary, 1923, indicates that she was then well-established. January lst reads '*Sheikh Abter Rahmin from Matruh visited the Industries - Much dyeing.*' Her much later article in 1959, describing her working environs, gives no hint of the social environ- ment in which she was then fully immersed. The picture which emerges from her diary however indicates that she had assistance from other English women: Miss Sawyer, Miss Pyeman, Mrs. Jones, and 'Gladys' all seem to be in- volved in her working life. The photograph of Violetta on a camel about to depart for Matruh to collect materials, at first seemed to indicate that this was her usual mode of transport. Her diary reveals that she frequently travelled to Cairo and Alexandria by train and car and to Matruh by boat on the *Sollum*. The diaries, in fact, reveal a wide variety of experiences and the true, quite busy, extent of her travels, just the tonic for a restless spirit.

Sometimes she sent her assistants to despatch carpets or collect materials, and several entries strike a despairing note.'*Could not get any warp.*' What the warp was for remains a mystery as the carpets woven in Burg were warp-faced wool and presumably spun by the Bedouins. Whether it was the raw fleece for making warps that was unavailable is not clear. An entry on January 3rd reads, '*Started General Hunter's shirt homespun.*'

The Industries received frequent visits from military personnel. General Hunter inspected the Industries and took Violetta to the Ministry of War to see the Minister Azmi Pasha for a discussion. She visited Matruh by boat and spoke to Captain Hillier about wool and the next day she saw Captain Green about wool. A Mr. de Halpert visited often and also inspected and made suggestions for the work at hand. A weaving school was opened on 19th April. It would appear that carpets were either exhibited or sent directly to the customer as an order. Exhibitions took place in Jerusalem, Ludd, Cairo and Alexandra. Bales were sent to Palestine and England.

Violetta maintained a busy social life at the same time. Her main companion was a Captain Deltman from the Sollum. They went for long walks, picked anemones and narcissi, played the gramophone and rode on his motor bike. They dined, wrote letters to one another, and generally enjoyed each other's company. At this point she was still celebrating her birthday on February 4th, although no one knew it was the day until she told Captain Deltman, who she referred to as CD or 'Capitano'.

In the middle of May, 1923 Violetta was taken ill and sent to hospital in Alexandria. Although obviously distressed with a fever she still managed to make entries in her diary. She remained in hospital for two weeks and Capitano visited most days. When discharged from hospital, she wrote '*came to stay with Mrs. Granville. Her mother, Mrs. Biddulph, is here. Dr. Granville away.*' Ierne Granville, Mrs. Biddulph, and another daughter, Norah, were to feature in Violetta's diaries for some years to come. Upon leaving Egypt for Europe on sick leave, Violetta purchased her ticket for the 22nd June, sailing on the SS Vienna to Venice. Her weight at this time was a tiny 6 stone, 8 pounds. Violetta left her car for Mrs. Granville to use while she was away on leave, and was seen onto the boat by Mrs. Granville, Mrs. Biddulph and Capitano. This is the last reference to Capitano in the diaries. (9)

The SS *Vienna* docked in Venice on June 25th. Violetta wrote, '*Got my letters. Had tea at the Grand Canal hotel and then went to the station----*' Thus began her journey to Danzig (Gdansk) to stay with the MacDonnells. She travelled through the Brennan Pass to Innsbruck, Munich, Nuremburg, where she changed some English money on June 27th-- '*Got 500,000 marks per one pound.*' She then left for Berlin and took the night train to Danzig. On June 29th she was turned off the train at 4 am at the Polish border for not having a Polish visa and was detained until 2 pm when she was allowed to proceed. There is no mention throughout this journey of her recent illness.

Violetta seemed to be marking time in Poland until she could join her brother Padge and his wife Tina in Cologne on July 7th. For the next ten days she was immersed in tennis parties, shopping, concerts, parties and bridge at the Polish Consulate and a general social round. Underlying all this, however, she noted the difficult political situations---

July 10th Padge very busy, conditions here very difficult. Violetta had written in her diary on July 9th, '*Came through the Ruhr, everything very desolate.*' The area had been invaded and occupied by French and Belgian forces on January 11th, 1923. They were met by passive resistance from the German workers and civilians had been killed by French soldiers. Germany's greatest industrial region came almost to a standstill and inflation galloped away. Violetta recorded, *July 21st Stayed in this morning and wrote article on the situation in Ruhr.*

On July 18th, Violetta notes, *Mr Ponsonby arrived from England. Paget new Vice Consul.*' She did not say where, but there is evidence that he was Vice consul in Genoa in 1927. Violetta left Cologne on the 24th July and had an *Interesting but tiresome journey to the Belgian frontier---Ticket fell out of the window.'*

Nevertheless, she arrived in London on the 25th having also lost her registered luggage. She stayed at the Wilton Hotel and made some visits, including one to Miss Grasett [10] The next morning she went to the CWL (Catholic Womens' League) and left the next day to go to Taunton where her registered luggage arrived on the 28th.

On the 13th August, Violetta's article for *The Spectator* was accepted. She re-let her cottage, saw the doctor who confirmed her sick leave until September 28th, and departed for Dublin. The holiday in Ireland seems to have been restful and she found the Irish to be delightful people. Back in England Dr. Baker extended her sick-leave for another 14 days and she spent these picnicking, picking blackberries and visiting the dog show. By 3rd October she was back in harness at Alexandria.

October 4th Went to the office this morning and saw Col. Parker for a long time and Major Farmer. Lunched with Major Farmer. Probabilities are that I go in the spring.' she spent several days in the office and had a long discussion with the Minister of War. On October 12th she went to Burg by train and was greeted by a nice welcome, *'very heart rending to have to tell them no more work.'* The next task was seeing the people, getting straight and finishing the scheme for the new school for Colonel Parker.

The next month was spent mostly at Burg, dyeing with lichens from the fig trees, trying the new alizarine colours, spinning, working in the office and arranging an exhibition at Burg which realised about three hundred pounds. *25th November Wrote another article for the Egyptian Horticultural Review.* The next exhibition was in Cairo. It seemed to do well and she lunched with Lord and Lady Allenby. On the 18th December Violetta was in Alexandria lunching with the Granvilles, returning to Burg on the next day *Loaded with warp and all the other things we wanted.* Ierne Granville and her sister went to stay the night in Burg on December

24

12th. This was the first time Norah (Bay) Biddulph had been mentioned in the diary. On 23rd December Violetta met Bay in Cairo, they visited the Tomb of the Marmelukes and then caught the night train to Luxor.

In 1922, the tomb of Tut-ankh-Amun was discovered at Luxor by Howard Carter and Lord Carnarvon. Violetta had the great good fortune to see the tomb before all its treasures were removed. Violetta's obituary in the *Cornwall Gazette*, elaborates on this Egyptian period stating that, 'She returned to England with a piece of shrine, later to be noted by the British Science Museum as part of the oldest shrine ever recorded.'[11] The museum does not hold the artifact. [12] Violetta also had in her collection of ancient textiles a 2000 year old piece of linen weaving from Luxor. [13]

In 1924 Violetta was recommended and accepted as a Fellow of the Royal Geographical Society (FRGS). Her credentials were given as Director of Bedouin Industries, Frontier Districts Administration and her address as El Burg El Arab, Maryut, Egypt. Her proposers were W. F. Hume, Director of the Geological Survey of Egypt and A. C. Parker.

Miss Thurstan has travelled extensively in the Balkan Peninsula, in Russia and Russian Poland. She has also camped for months in tents in the Canada Mountains in Tenerife, and lived in the mining districts of Southern Spain and East Portugal. Has also been to Suia and Baharia Oases, to Tripoli frontier, Spain and Palestine. Has always been interested in Geography and took that subject as one for the L.L.A. Diploma of St. Andrews University. Has published a book about Russia and numerous travel articles.[14]

She resigned from this Society in 1930. No reason was given. A wry remark was made by a relative that "perhaps she could not afford to keep up the subscriptions." The archivist of the RGS offers the suggestion that 'perhaps, if she was still travelling, she decided it was not worth belonging to a London Society.' Violetta's diaries indicate that from at least 1929 onwards, she was resident in England and

25

travelled to London frequently. Unless she had private means, the former reasoning may be nearer the mark.

There is no evidence to indicate when Violetta left Egypt, but there are hearsay references to her advising on the crafts in Albania in 1927, and to her walking in the Pyrenees in 1928. The next factual evidence comes from the 1929 diary which records her living with Norah Biddulph (Bay) at Dragon House in the village of Washford near Minehead in Somerset. Hubert Fox, Norah's biographer, [15] has recorded the information that Norah came from an Anglo-Irish family, went to stay in Egypt with her sister Ierne who married a doctor, Alexander Granville. Norah found a job at Bourg el Arab where Bedouin women were taught to spin and weave, 'Norah and another English woman being in charge.' Her job came to an end in 1924 and Norah then went to Sweden to take courses in spinning and weaving. Then she began spinning, weaving and bottling fruit with an acquaintance (Violetta) at Dragon House. If Violetta also left Egypt in 1924, it is difficult to account for her seven years with the Bedouins as the length of time often quoted for her stay there.

Throughout 1929, Violetta and Bay were involved in village life, making various forays to London and Sussex. It seems that Bay's family base was at Warnham near Horsham, and she and Violetta used it as a jumping off place when they were in that part of the country.

In 1924 Violetta's 'Articles on Dyeing' were published by the *Egyptian Horticultural Review*. Five years later, on December 16, 1929, she noted in her diary *Sent off my dye book to Dryad.....*' This book, *Use of Vegetable Dyes for Beginners*, published in 1930, was to prove a best seller. [16] Still in print today, it is a standard text for all those wishing to acquaint themselves with the art of natural dyes. A small book of approximately 50 pages, it is a simply and concisely written recipe book, and has been described by Betty Jackson, author of *Growing Herbs and Plants for Dyeing* as a 'no nonsense practical little book'. Violetta Thurstan is probably remembered more for this book than any other event in her long life. Having said this, she was not the first to write a recipe book of dyes. She was entering the well-established craft scene which had arisen from the Arts and Crafts Movement in the 19th century and was influenced by the work of William Morris. In the early part of the 20th century, like-minded craftsmen and women lived and worked in communities, forming Handicraft Guilds and Societies. Ethel Mairet [17], an influential figure in the weaving and dyeing world, was involved in the communities in Chipping Camden, initially with her first husband, Ananda Coomaraswarmy, and later in Ditchling with her second husband, Phillip Mairet.

Like Violetta, Ethel Mairet travelled extensively, mainly in India, Ceylon and Europe and had amassed a significant collection of textiles. In 1916 she had written *Vegetable Dyes*, and in the 11th edition of 1952, the year of her death, she wrote 'It (*Vegetable Dyes*) has remained the chief book on the subject in English, although some less comprehensive ones have been written.' Violetta and Ethel Mairet did meet. On June 10, 1929, Violetta was staying in Warnham and arranged to visit friends in Hampshire. On the way she made a detour. Her diary reads, '*Went to Ditchling, first to Mrs. Mairet then to Mr. Kilbride.*' '*Very interesting*' reads her diary, a comment which sheds nothing on the nature of the meeting or the relationship.

p. 28 Violetta in the 1920s.

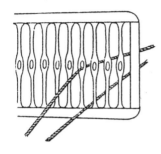

Chapter 5

Living and weaving

At the end of July, 1929, Violetta and Bay went off to Scandinavia for six weeks. The house in Somerset was let to a Miss Phillips. The two friends were plaiting in Norway and weaving in Sweden. They also spent time walking and sightseeing. On August 19th, Violetta writes that *'Began a snaljerug and have nearly finished my wall hanging. My eyes have been troublesome and couldn't work all the time'*. There are other references throughout the years to eye problems.

In the middle of October Violetta and Bay were exhibiting and demonstrating in London at the Imperial Institute. The exhibition lasted for five days and was a huge success. *'Crowds of people.' 'Very busy day, people surging in by thousands.'* Still they managed to enjoy a lively social life. *'Tonight dined with Ierne and then we went to Bernard Shaw's new play, Apple Cart. Terribly good.' 'Dined with Ierne and then we went to a most exciting film, Four Feathers.'*

29

Back in Somerset the end of the year brought damaging gales which devastated their trees and curtailed their outings. Bay went to Warnham for Christmas and after Christmas Violetta with Danny, her dog, joined her. Returning to Somerset, Violetta continued teaching and writing articles.

January 17 Went with Bay to see Persian Exhibition which took our hearts away it was so beautiful.

January 23 Article for Home & county came out (Sweden). They returned photographs.

March 2nd Went to Heals about rugs. Fairly satisfactory.

At the end of March Violetta and Bay went to stay with Padge and Tina in Genoa. A note in her diary, *Great news in one paper, King Alphonso of Spain abdicated and Catalonia declared itself a republic.* [1] Back in England, on May 18th, 1931 Violetta and Bay were getting ready for the Bath and West Show. The Show was not successful from a selling point of view and the weather was poor. *Left in the pouring rain. Fetched things from a sea of mud. Puncture on the way.* In addition to weaving lessons, Violetta was giving private lessons in German, Spanish, French and Italian. She was also busy with her own weaving and dyeing.

In June Violetta was off to tour Finland returning on the 21st to be met by Bay in Bath. Once again they were negotiating to let the house, and this seems to have been a further and regular source of income. Soon after Violetta left for the Isle of Wight where *'Lady Simeon's car met me'*. The next day she spent judging at a small show of work. In August Violetta entertained her family. They celebrated her Father's 80th birthday. The Taunton Flower Show was on the 12th and 13th of August that summer and proved successful for the two friends. They sold many rugs and some tweeds. Having let the house to a Captain Anson for six months, Violetta and Bay headed for Warnham on the 15th and Violetta began a weaving course at Westerham, between Redhill and Sevenoaks.

To provide a background catalogue of Violetta's involvement with her craft, the following is a complete section from her diary during the weaving course. It gives some insight into Violetta's relationships with her contemporaries. She refers to them as 'they', and seemed relieved when the course was over. Some names mentioned were to recur in later diaries.

August 17th Made a design but no loom available. Learnt spinning on a spindle (Miss Peacock).

August 18th Got on to drawloom and did a design of birds and tree. Lecture on dyeing tonight.

August 19th Did some dyeing this morning

August 20th Made designs-no loom available. Lecture by one Miss Milne(?, VT's question) on Central African mats. Did some dyeing this a.m.

August 21st Nothing much to do today. Made designs. A kind of party tonight and I had to be a palmist.

August 22nd They had a sort of At Home this aft. A lot of people came including Luther Hooper. I began a piece of work on Mrs. Cooper's loom & made a design of little stags.

August 23rd Mrs. Whitelaw kindly took me to church at Sevenoaks in her car. Afterwards I worked at Mrs. Cooper's loom all day.

August 24th Finished my piece on Mrs. Cooper's loom. Most of the day was teaching Miss Somervil how to weave tapestry.

August 25th Poured all day. Very cold-Mr. Inderwick gave a discourse on more interesting pattern weaving on 4 pedal looms.

August 26th Miss Preece came and gave a very interesting lecture on Old Textiles. Not quite as wet as yesterday but very cold.

August 27th Couldn't have loom today! Miss Henderson & I went into the village to buy some presents for Mrs. Thompson at the Farm.

August 28th Tomorrow we finish. Did a bit on little draw loom. Got ready a bit of tablet weaving to show them tonight. The Skilbecks came but did not meet them.

August 29th Last day of Course. Rather glad to finish for several reasons. Bay and Mrs. Biddulph came to fetch me. [2]

Elizabeth Peacock was a lecturer on this course and it is of interest that in 1931, Miss Peacock was the co-founder of the first Guild of Weavers, Spinners and Dyers, together with its journals and summer schools. It is possible that the course which Violetta attended was a prototype summer school. This was also the time when Miss Peacock was spinning and dyeing her fleece for the Dartington Banners, and just before she began working with drawlooms.

Hilda Breed [3] in her article on Dorothy Wilkinson [4] talks about the Guild of Drawloom Weavers among whom were Aristede Messenisi, Alice Hindson [5], Sandeman Allen and Mrs. Cooper, all pupils of Luther Hooper. Hooper and Messenisi with the help of Waldo Lanchester, the great puppet exponent, succeeded in erecting a drawloom capable of weaving a repeat pattern 24" wide. From Violetta's descriptions of her designs and references to Mrs. Cooper's loom and the visit of Luther Hooper, it would indicate that this was a course with a drawloom element.

In September they returned to Minehead and appeared to be living in a house called 'Hopscott.' *September 1st We have dug ourselves in so nicely here and are going to have a lovely little studio. Sorted ? Got storeroom and dressing room ready. Bay did kitchen, etc.* The following day Violetta saw Dr. Meade King, about her arm, on her way to a Women's Institute meeting where she was speaking on Finland. He thought her condition was serious and a series of X-rays and the diagnosis of a TB shoulder then followed. Violetta was told not to use her right arm again *'so must learn to write with left'.* She continued teaching weaving and Italian until she entered a nursing home to have her arm put in plaster. Obviously she was in a lot of pain. *'Rotten night. Can't stand this plaster case very well but Mr. Groves is away for the weekend. Gladys came to see me this afternoon and Bay came back this evening. Thanks be.'* In the midst of all this pain she writes, *'Bad news in the paper. Stock Exchange closed. Bank rate up 6%.'*

Violetta continued to have a number of visitors even after she left the nursing home. Bay's Mother and sister Ethne arrived to stay for a few days and Violetta commented, *'How kind everyone is.'* Nevertheless, throughout this period her diary reminds us that she continued to teach languages and give lectures locally. On October 31st Mr. Groves pronounced himself satisfied with Violetta's arm so she and Bay went up to London on the 3.15, stayed at the Club, dined and lunched with Ierne, and saw *'a terrific play, Port Said- one most sordid ever seen.'* They returned home after visiting the Exhibition at Burlington House.

In following Violetta's story over the next two years, there is some discrepancy in dates, and a break in the continuity of the diaries. Hubert Fox, writing about the Quantock Weavers in 1934, tells the story of Norah Bidulph and Gladys Dickinson. He reports that Gladys went to join Norah (Bay) and her acquaintance (Violetta) at Dragon House in 1932, following which Gladys and Bay had taken the lease of the Old Forge, Plainsfield, a rambling old house with outhouses and a courtyard. At the Old Forge, which was close to the Quantock Hills in Somerset, they set up business together, spinning, weaving and bottling fruit. [6] The date discrepancy arises because in Violetta's 1934 diary, she seems to indicate that Bay's departure was quite recent.

Her diary entry for 1 January, 1934 is full of disasters.*Began this year Dragon Cottage Minehead. Came downstairs at 10 to midnight New Year's Eve. Found kitchen fire out and bath overflowed into back regions, so began New Year mopping. Joan Henderson left 10 days ago. Miss Brahmer from Sweden in here to finish up orders and Miss Bell is here as pupil for a week. Bay is as she was. Went to Mass early and then went to Nether Stowey and on to Plainsfield. No luck.*

Though there is no extensive information about this broken relationship, this must have been a very traumatic time for Violetta. Although it appears that Violetta had been the major breadwinner for the two companions, Bay had been the car driver. For the rest of life Violetta had to rely on others for her transport. Violetta did not seem to bear malice, though information is necessarily sketchy, and she continued to note Bay's birthday in her diary up to 1938.

After a visit to Italy, to see Padge and Tina, Violetta made references to 'taking people on'. She engaged Ruth Foulds on trial for a month, at the end of which she remarked that Ruth did not accept the post, but stayed around for a while. Rae Castle, who was to give dressmaking classes, then appears in diary entries. This was the year that *A Short History of Decorative Textiles* was published. One paragraph from Violetta's Foreword illustrates her own feelings related to the art of weaving, and justifies her strong interest in and commitment to it. [7]

The history of textiles embraces every conceivable human activity, births and deaths and marriages, rustic, urban and maritime interests, the history of nations, and the gentle dalliance of love. Weaver and Webster are two of the commonest surnames and every unmarried woman is a spinster in the eye of the law. Thus it is with more than common interest that the history of weaving is unfolded, it is in fact the history of the human race.

In May Violetta was indignant about a factory inspector who called and went over the house because she said it was a factory. No further mention was made to the visit or outcome. Shortly after, Violetta's Father and Aunt Lou arrived for a few days, while she was '*feverishly getting ready for the Bath & West Show.*' Other shows which she attended included Torquay and Frome, and in October she had a stand in Chelsea Town Hall.

June found Violetta in London at a V&A exhibition, after which she returned to Corsham where she was sorting the Library. Corsham appears frequently in Violetta's early diaries and is still mentioned in 1952 when was apparently still 'doing' the Library. She mentions Lady Methuen staying there. A letter to her brother, Padge, detailing her will in 1934 is on Corsham Court notepaper, and Bobbie Cox, an eminent tapestry weaver today, gives an account of Violetta in the early 1950s which confirms this Corsham connection.

It was late '40s, early '50s and we were students at the Bath Academy at Corsham. We lived at Monks Park on the Weston Road and biked past her house at the end of the South Avenue every day. It had big gates, always shut. 'They said' she dyed in the yard, dark blue. 'They said she wove things' and that her dyes came from plants. She was old. We never saw her. We imagined this strange lady doing strange things behind the gate and in that big old house. We never dared peep over the gate. We were dedicated students of painting and sculpture weaving and dyeing and sculpture, weaving and dyeing were things we would never be interested in. So the old lady never came into our lives, and later how much I have regretted never meeting her. [8]

Later she visited Rae Castle's family in Bournemouth and remarked that *'It is practically settled that Rae shall come as partner.'* [9] The two returned with a small puppy called Judy who was ill. By the end of the year Grizel, another dog, was acquired.   Violetta and Rae went to Scandinavia at the end of July, and one of the places they stayed was Mora. This may have been where Violetta found her peasant weave illustrated in *Weaving Without Tears.* [10] Two visits were made to the Isle of Wight to judge their show. Mr. Merheim arrived in September and spent a week 'busy dyeing'. Germain Merheim was a research chemist who worked out a simple method for dyeing vat colours.

When the V&A acknowledged a piece of weaving given by Violetta in 1935, her address is listed as Dragon House,

Bookay Down, Kingswear, South Devon. This second Dragon House rather adds to the confusion, but she must have liked the name and taken it with her.

By the end of November, Violetta was in Winchester and first mentions that she is making pottery. Who she was with or what she was making is unknown but she *painted pottery and sat up with the kiln until 2.30am.* Later when Violetta was living in Penryn, Cornwall, Margaret Way remembers her in attendance at Falmouth pottery classes.

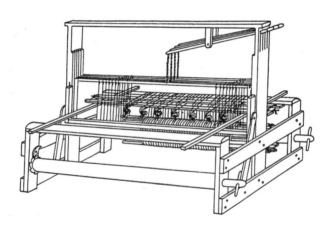

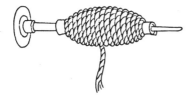

Chapter 6

And more war

The Spanish Civil War began in July 1936 in Morocco. The core of the Nationalist Army came from the African Army led by General Franco. In 1937 he incorporated the Falange, seized control, and appealed directly to Hitler and Mussolini for help. Although the Western governments protested, they did nothing and victory began to swing to the Fascists who had greater supplies of weapons and had united their followers through political propaganda. Only the Soviet Union offered help. After the German bombing of Guernica in April 1937, all the Western democracies isolated Spain.

A month later, on the 31st May, German warships shelled Almeria in reprisal for the bombing of their ship the *Deutschland*. Almeria, a small town on the southern coast of Spain, was put under siege, and Violetta was there. In her view she was on the wrong side. [1] She did not make a public stand of any kind but quietly set about releasing prisoners. The authors have been unable to find out why

55-year old Violetta was there or even in what capacity, but after the siege was lifted, she and others were declared *persona non grata*'and expelled from Spain. [2] It has been estimated that a million people died or emigrated from Spain during the Civil War.

Violetta began 1938 in her studio in Paignton, Devon. She went to Corsham Court in early January where she resumed work on the library, and while there she mentions *Batsford's offer re Decorative Textiles*. This refers to the offer Batsford made to reprint her book. In a signed first edition copy of it dated 1942 she has altered Pepler and Sewell's name (the original publishers) to Batsford. [3]

On March 3rd she went to London for a meeting about the Handloom Weavers Society at the home of Mrs. Ford Anderson where about 14 others were also there. Soon after, she reports grave news in her diary, *from Austria, Schuschnigg has resigned.'* [4] Kurt von Schuschnigg had taken over as Chancellor of Austria from the murdered Dolfuss and was trying to resist Austrian Naziism.

At the end of April the Committee of the Devon Art Society met in Violetta's studio and toward the end of May she was preparing for the Plymouth Show and the Bath & West Show. Once more the latter proved to be very wet and cold. At the end of May she was in Cologne, heading for Goteberg and Oslo, seemingly on a sight-seeing trip. She returned via Stockholm, Copenhagen and Berlin, and on her arrival back she met Dorothy Wilkinson and told her of the Berlin exhibition she had seen. On that same day she attended a committee meeting of the Arts and Crafts Exhibition Society.

Her concerns about the war began to increase. *15th September Foreign news bad. Trouble in Czechoslovakia* Two weeks later, *Plans for evacuating all children and old people from London.* She recorded Chamberlain's visit to Munich, and on Wednesday, 28th September, Violetta heard that the Women's Territorial Army was launched. She abandoned everything and rushed into Exeter to offer her services. For the next four days she began enrolling members using the Fourth Devons Regimental Drill Hall. when the crisis died down she returned to her weaving, judging, writing and visiting friends and colleagues. Central Hall, Westminster, was the venue of the next Exhibition and sale, a six day event beginning at the end of October. During the week she gave a lecture on pattern and design.

With the invasion of Poland in 1939, Britain and France declared war on Germany. Violetta immediately volunteered and joined the WRNS with responsibilities for educational duties. At this time she gave her date of birth as 4th February 1890, declaring herself eleven years younger than she was. On her first S206 report, she loses yet another year and on the latest form held by the Ministry of Defence she declares herself to be 47 years old, when she was, in fact, 62. [5]

January, 1940, found Violetta in Cornwall. During the next 12 months, she travelled the length and breadth of England and Scotland recruiting, setting up centres, organizing and giving lectures in the course of her duties with the Admiralty. While working with the Naval Intelligence in Falmouth, she helped with the inspection of ships coming from Holland, Greece, Denmark, Norway, Portugal, Italy and Argentina. In her diary are recorded comments such as, *a big mine explosion -- phosphorous from seized ship sent for analysis -- pouring with rain -- sea rough -- nice Captain but a dirty little ship loaded with fish meal -- great agitation over the Norwegian expedition -- too rough to go out today.*

On the 20th March, the Duke of Kent inspected the unit and a photograph was taken of him with Violetta and Captain Hutchings. Between 10 May and the 21st of the month she recorded that, *Germany invaded Holland and Belgium for the second time - News bad - Refugees to England - 300 in a boat -- Germans take Anas and Amiens -- played rounders.*

The reader gets a picture of pure indifference to personal comfort and an almost frantic whirl of activity. Outside official duties, she organized hockey and chess matches for the Wrens, helped with a Naval concert and show, attended the cinema and local dances, gave lectures and relaxed by maintaining a full social programme of lunches, dinners and overnight stays with friends. This was a very full life, especially for a woman in her sixties. Throughout the war years Violetta also maintained her committment to weaving. She organised craft rooms in the various barracks and dockyards which she visited and invited Dorothy Wilkinson from the London School of Weaving to teach weaving to the WRNS and WAAF in North Wales and Scotland.

The Admiralty sent her to Dover 'for some secret work' and on June 11th, Italy declared war. She had to go *down a cellar whilst explosives shook the house*' then travelled on to Broadstairs to start '*a new station with a wireless, 3 Wrens for operations and 2 for staff.* The job involved finding accommodation, organizing the delivery of all essentials and the training and setting up of operations. She repeated this exercise in Brighton, Harwich, Eastbourne, Isle of Wight and in Cornwall at the Lizard, Coverack and Mullion. Her comments read, *found a suitable site -- and during air raid, Wrens and beds arrived (Portsmouth) -- rather weary after 36 hours up (Eastbourne) -- got about 20 quite good candidates (Isle of Wight) -- took night watch again (Mullion) -- entertained Australian press (Portsmouth) -- very bad bombing -- my bed covered with debris and broken glass -- a very bad night of air raids -- people thought invasion was imminent.*

She travelled to Blythe, Whitley Bay, Newcastle, then back to Gloucester and Devizes, *rather a good place for recruiting* up to Edinburgh, North Berwick and Carlisle, where *sprained ankle very swollen and painful.* Yet two days later she was off to Oban and despite *a very bad cold and temperature and sorry for myself* was nevertheless busy with interviewing candidates. Her recruiting, often done through the Labour exchanges covered the Perth and Dumfries area. As a devout Catholic she went to Mass '*early, if possible, Church crowded with Poles*'. On December

20th she left Carlisle for Taunton for a short Christmas break.

Commander Margaret Cole [6] WRNS of the Directorate of Naval Officer Appointments has given a resume of Violetta's service. Placed together with information sent from the Royal Naval College, Greenwich [7], these records form part of Appendix II. Violetta's own summary of her work was stated in a letter to the Imperial War Museum, dated 30 May, 1977, is included in the same appendix.

During her time at HMS Drake Violetta was appointed to both administrative duties and 'special duties' which indicates that she worked in Intelligence where her knowledge of foreign languages could be employed. Falmouth had a Contraband Control Base, ' which boasted a unique personality in the person of 1st officer VT who was later well known in the service as an O.T.C. Staff Officer and an Education Lecturer.'

Vera Laughton Mathews (later Dame), the author of Blue Tapestry quoted above, and the Director of WRNS (Women's Royal Naval Service) from 1939-1946, concluded her remarks about Violetta in the following summary,

' She spoke every known tongue and - her job at Falmouth was to accompany a naval officer on board the foreign merchant ships and engage the skipper in entertaining conversation, (while) the naval officer rifled his cabin. It seemed a job made for her.'[8]

Mary Barker also gives a graphic description of meeting Violetta at the WRNS officer training college at Greenwich (9),

' My first meeting with Violetta Thurstan was at the Royal Naval College, Greenwich, during the Second World War. At morning parade the first day, a WRNS Officer rushed into place a little late carrying a small white dog under one arm. As candidates for commission we all had to appear extremely neat in correct uniform on every occasion (even air raids) so our eyes opened wide as both lady

41

and dog had wispy white hair that moulted over navy uniform. Obviously an exception to the general rule was being made for someone special. Violetta's naval career must have been a trial to the WRNS high command. Besides parades and drill we had to attend lectures on current affairs as well as on specialized naval subjects. These were given by distinguished visiting lecturers, all male except for 1st Officer Thurstan. She was brilliant; her subject was desert warfare in Egypt and the great Western Desert which stretches hundreds of miles before it merges into the Sahara.

She was good at obtaining resources and influencing decisions, and she enjoyed working directly with those in charge, then organising and supporting individuals and groups. All of this required planning, resourcefulness and travel. Her lectures on a multitude of subjects extended her work far beyond her service brief, and she was willing to speak to Girl Guides, Brains Trust gatherings and Women's Institute meetings to stimulate awareness and abilities. Exhibitions, handicrafts, talks, lectures, all of these were aimed at helping morale in a time of disruption by bombs, regulations, deprivations and emotional uncertainties.

Violetta had dashed to and fro, from Aberdeen to Grimsby, Holyhead to Kirkwall, Cardiff to Tobermory, but always holding London, the HMS Naval Base, Rosyth and Cornwall as the three fixed points of security, her friends, her base and her home. These short breaks were very important as they helped her to relax. Her diary entries record a catalogue of places, times, people, engagements. They rarely refer to difficulties except briefly such as a 'long wet journey', 'took drifter to Kirkwall', 'slight accident with car', 'air raid rather noisy' and other minor annoyances.

She was always eager to learn and was sent on courses, as well as serving on social welfare committees. At Rosyth she was appointed to the Social Welfare Council. Commander Baxter introduced her to the Regional Committee at St. Andrews, and after the war he became one of their professors. Violetta visited there on several occasions.

42

In January, 1944 her job was taken over by another colleague and the focus of her work had gone. In February her much-loved sister-in-law, Tina, died. Violetta switched her energies again into setting up handicraft centres, '*new H craft room for the Wrens at St. Leonards*', '*Handicraft club formed in Newcastle*', '*Technical School wants the looms*', '*a beautiful room at Pitraine Castle*'. She was drifting, however, and her widowed brother, Padge, suggested she join him for two months. Since all leave had been cancelled this did not prove possible. Nevertheless, a short time later she met Lady Elgin who introduced her to the Curator of the National Gallery, she visited the Chinese Exhibition, and she got some royalties from Dryads. In July, uncertainties came to a head and Violetta was suddenly required to move her office and wasn't pleased with the new one. With 49 others she travelled in a luggage van to London through flying bombs and visited Falmouth where her friend, Hattie, told her that the Pentargon Hotel had been destroyed in the last raid.

The unconditional surrender of Germany was received in 1944. In Alamagordo, New Mexico, the Americans triggered the first atomic explosion, followed by President Truman's approval for the bombing of Hiroshima and Nagasaki. Violetta remained in post, and then after an eight month spell as the Education Officer on HMS Cochrane II, aged 65, she asked to be released.

The war years had imposed enormous strain on everyone, but it was generally believed that victory was just a matter of time. The uncertainty, of course, was exactly when? The Allies were deploying all resources toward the planned final invasion. Over the previous four years Violetta had displayed a degree of resilience and energy that fired the imagination of those with whom she worked. Everything did not always go smoothly but she was noted for her interest in people, for making quick contacts and for always being prepared to move immediately to the unexpected.

The year long difficulties resulted in Violetta's application to UNRRA (United Nations Relief and Rehabilitation Association) for a post, and on October 10th, she went to Cathedral Welfare League for an interview where she was accepted '*probably for the Balkans.*' She proceeded to hand in her notice, with no explanation, and four days later learned that her release had come through. '*I leave the Navy with many regrets on October 21st.*' [10] She was scheduled to work for the Catholic Committee for Relief Abroad and '*to be in charge of a party.*' Inoculated and suffering reaction she '*had a long talk with the Duchess of Kent*' before going from Rosyth to Cornwall, where '*after a flurry of activity*', she left Liverpool by boat on the 8th November, arriving at St. Joseph's, Cairo on 22nd November.

The next month was spent in taking lessons in Serbian, attending orientation lectures, sorting out money, visiting and dining with colleagues, while attending the Cairo General Purpose Committee meetings. She took her meals at the New Zealand Club and used the American UNRRA Centre. She had also taken over the duties of a Miss O'Donnell, checking Serbian records.

p. 44 Contraband control Falmouth. Violetta with Duke of Kent and Captain Hutchings.

Chapter 7

Gathering loose ends

The surge of responsibility for relief work in the immediate aftermath of the war resulted in uncoordinated centres of humanitarian support. The task was enormous.

Violetta, Dr. Edith Coleman, and others worked through agencies such as The Save the Children Fund, the Red Cross Society, The Society of Friends and, locally to Violetta, the Cairo Council, to push forward the Catholic Relief Programme. All schemes had to process through various military units: French, British, American, Russian. Violetta flew to Naples, *very cold and dirty and no hot water'*, taking the train to Bari to meet the team, *'a very interesting lecture from liaison officer just back from Yugoslavia. It does not sound a happy country.'*[1] She flew to Rome, reported, and then had an encounter with thieves, *'stealing from a car and they broke my finger.'* She saw 400 refugees in Porte Aurelia and had her first private audience with the Holy Father, the Pope, on Sunday, 28th January, 1945.

Back in Cairo she received a summons from Mrs. Woodruff to return to Rome. After several 'stormy meetings' she arrived back only to discover no Mrs. Woodruff. She used the time to find a house, owned by the Countess Giumezza Savelli at Acuto which *would accommodate 40-50 children*. *'We would be free of UNRRA to some extent.'* *'Rations will not be impossible to get.'* Her plans for the house did not materialise but after the war the house was used as a training centre for nursery students. When Mrs. Woodruff eventually arrived on the 26th, Violetta spent ten days with her before returning on the 9th March to Egypt.

Ten days later she was totally immersed in local politics, trying to organise food, bedding, clothing and cotton to be sent to Italy and holding interviews with Barclays Bank about the account book, before flying back to Rome for April consultations. She notes that *'Tito will not accept any relief workers for Jug-o-Slavia.'* From her new office at 231 Corso Umberto on Tuesday, May 8th, she recorded the excellent news *'Peace in Europe declared. Churchill 3 pm. the King at 9 pm.'*

On June 1st she had a letter asking her to go to Tripoli about repatriating Italian children. She went to UNRRA but *'they won't play'*. Undeterred she went to the British Consulate and the Civil Affairs branch and got authorization, leaving her able to depart on the 8th for Benghazi, Castel Benito, with a final 17 mile drive into Tripoli. There she found the Hotel Del Mehari *very nice*.

At the Military Administration Headquarters in Tripoli she met officials and finally got the permissions she needed. She then took an aeroplane to Rome, delivered the positive reports to a Major J and Monsignor K then lunched with a Contessa. Ten days in Rome followed filled with socialising and relaxing before learning about an injured colleague and travelling to Uding to see her. In two days there she visited the Polish Transit Camp and saw people returning from Slave Labour Camps in Germany. These were women with small babies, everyone in rags, vitamin starvation rampant, no books, no drugs, no medical comforts of any kind. Later that week she visited the Austrian Commission.

Soon she was back in Cairo where she found Bishop Hughes eager for her to help in the evacuation of Egyptian children. Violetta then went to Tripoli and together with Brigadier Blackley, Colonel Mercer and Captain Russell they prepared a list of 119 children. Nevertheless Violetta still found time to visit a bazaar and buy wool.

She flew to Klagenfurt in Austria via Malta and spent the morning with the Austrian Commission before returning to Rome. After a second audience with the Holy Father she returned to Austria to meet Colonel Logan Grey who was setting up the Catholic Relief Agency. He became an important friend to Violetta. She was taken to the Slovakian Camp at Treviso and when she gave them gifts they became very emotional. She visited Polish and Italian camps before returning to Rome.Back in Tripoli she found the children waiting for a ship, and difficulties being made by Major J about Italian nurses accompanying the children. Nevertheless, on 18th August, the nurses, the children and Violetta were given Audience with the Holy Father.

Dr. Coleman was delegated to accompany the Egyptian children to Bari. Four days later, Violetta was summoned to London, and after a short break in Falmouth she returned to Rome taking insulin to Monsignor Tardini at the Vatican. She then organised the departure of the second batch of children from Centocelli. All of this work Violetta records succinctly, 'I did hospital work with foreign refugees in Egypt and then an eight month period working for the Catholic Committee for Relief Abroad'. [2] The Vatican had been established as an independent state in 1929. Violetta had arranged the evacuation of 100 Italian children to North Africa using a British Naval ship, and the Pope recognised her contribution by making her a Companion of the Vatican.

Her next assignment was to the Klagenfurt Camp in Austria, where the Catholics were invited to take over the camps in Vienna filled with Sudeten Germans and Volks Deutsch. She found them in shocking condition. Later the camps were condemned and moved into one British section. Major Chapman asked her '*to contact Salzburg UNRRA about getting goods from Egypt.*' Back in Rome she saw the Holy Father with the Tripoli children, attended the Pontifical Commission and helped to organize the accounts for the Austrian fund. Difficulties and misunderstandings regularly arose between the four allies and their voluntary organisations. Some complexity related to refugee work delayed Violetta's immediate departure. She used the time to get herself innoculated, lunched with prestigious friends such as the Princess Dana, the Marchessa Cavalcanti and the Countessa Aldo Brandisi, and generally exploited the unexpected break.

Finally the children left on the 22nd October, and with confirmation of her next appointment, she left immediately for Austria. She spent time delivering letters and parcels from Roman relatives to Baroness Von Archenburgh, the Countess Esterhazy and called on the Bishop to leave '*a few comforts.*' Interviewed by General McLeod and Brigadier Armitage, the camp was inspected. She went to Kappel Camp, visited the baby clinic and was asked for handicraft material and books for the Scheifling Camp. Colonel Hall '*approves of CCRA personnel being sent here and showed me his letter to Lady Falmouth.*' By early November the arrangements were complete. She returned, '*I had a hair-raising journey over the high mountain pass without any lights*' and settled to work at Klagenfurt and at the Scheifling Camp, where her responsibility was for the children.

It often happens that when danger threatens systems work well, but it sometimes occurs that things collapse and fall apart. Local rivalries become obvious and only good sense and determination can re-establish order. Violetta frequently used the Greek word 'bulimia' (state of exhaustion caused by starvation and cold) to express conditions in the camps as she continued to seek support directly from Rome officials, and patiently push forward with improvements. '*Quarantine barracks opened*', '*Orthopaedic ward finished*', '*Gymnasium begun*' and '*toy factory*' are the phrases which pepper her diaries. The RAF constantly brought gifts of supplies and carried parcels back and forth, helpers came and left, '*all very complicated and difficult.*'

Routines were established, regular meals and diets monitored, and Violetta also worked on recreational programmes to attempt to balance the medical support being given. An operetta was performed, handicraft centres established, looms found, embroidery lessions started and a gift shop opened where the products, made by patients, could be sold to the many visitors who called. Chaos is hinted at throughout, '*Italian chauffeur more stupid than can be imagined, decided to come by train and leave him.*, '*conference on the difficulties one German doctor was making*'. But she also reports on the beauties of the countryside, takes walks with her dog Timsie, goes to dances, sees the film, *National Velvet*, at the YMCA and joins in the social life of the officers. Frequently she visited Vienna and her many friends made through her initial delivery of mail and parcels from Rome.

By April she was exhausted, and '*Mr. Nutterall wants me to take a few days sick leave.*' On the 16th she left for Rome but her sick leave appears to have involved a '*dance for about 600, helped with refreshments.*'

Returning to camp she learned that the Austrian government was now in a position to take over the running of it, and that Scheifling could close. Austria had a superb record for helping refugees. Violetta and the others continued their work. Patients came and left, displaced persons arrived, were processed and moved on. In between '*hopping back and forth to Rome*' she hints at difficulties as the staff who, whilst welcoming changes, often had genuine problems in adapting. '*With great trouble got Miss X to move out of her room. Have it for my office temporarily, but it is too small.'*

She organized *'an exhibition of things'* in Vienna. *'A bogus naval lieutenant came. We were completely taken in, gave him supper and a bed for the night.' 'My suitcase stolen at the Russian frontier. Second time this month.' 'Probably moving to Leoben for winter.'* On October 9th she returned to London, her ankle having been injured and quite painful. Three days later she travelled to Penryn.

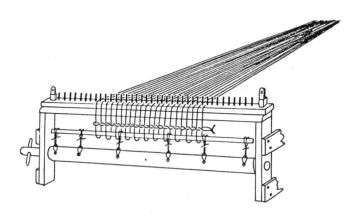

Chapter 8

Tieing the knots

Violetta could never be still for long. Declaring herself to be a mere fifty-four years 'young' she went before a selection board and enrolled for service in the Department of POW's and Displaced Persons (DP's), an organization set up by the Allied Commission at the end of the war. She joined the British section responsible to the Foreign & Commonwealth Office [1] where she worked continuously for the next 25 months before finally being made redundant in November, 1948.

Though her continual changes of age may be questionable, checks were obviously casual. She was operating largely in a man's world at a time when it was considered ungallant to query the age of a lady. The post-war years were a time of utter confusion. By listing her latest contribution to the war effort, coupled with her ability to seek out the unexpected, she would have been gratefully accepted by overworked officials. Violetta wish to serve. If that meant altering her age, so be it!

Violetta could be overbearing, and it is easy to understand how. Her range of experiences by 1947 made her formidable. Most colleagues considered her to be generous, firm but unsympathetic to those she felt 'did not meet the mark.' She made no excuses for her terse comments or irritated rejections of individuals found lacking. She never apologised whatever the circumstances and sometimes she failed to give credit to those who did not possess the same vision, physical or mental stamina. Her support for her own team and for those officials with whom she felt in tune was absolute. She pushed herself to the limit to cajole, improve and create a warm atmosphere for the patients, rewarding people with many manifestations of kindness and small gifts. Her correspondence was by now voluminous with acquaintances, dignitaries and former colleagues met along her way. Nevertheless she still found time to continue with her own writing for publication.

'(I) was in charge of a hospital for refugees and displaced people in Austria, practically no food, heating, bedding or any other supplies were available.'[2] The main work of the Department was to assist in the Repatriation of Refugees and POW's back to their original homelands, a task made doubly difficult by the realignment of national boundaries and the thousands of people involved. The United Nations was set up clearly defining the principles that an exhausted world wished to adopt. Documents from the Society of Friends, Israel, and various humanitarian groups, voluntary agencies and letters from individuals starkly compliment the official records held by European governments. Their factual analysis listing the immensity of the devastation can still give a shudder to a reader of history today. The phenomenal waste of human talent and psychological effect of oppression on the disenfranchised must have made every volunteer into a determined radical. 'Deeds not words are what count' said Violetta.

She was based with the DP Division ACA (Displaced persons division of the Allied Commission for Austria) in Klagenfurt where she met past Catholic Welfare League colleagues and found Colonel Logan Grey once more in charge. The Red Cross nurses were getting ready to transfer to Treffly and the massive movement of refugees almost overwhelmed resources. The intense period of biting cold and snow of the winter and spring of 1947 added considerably to difficulties.

'Road icy, driver killed', 'leave one week to Rome, 20 Jan CCNA', 'renew all contacts.' Back in Austria she visited Waidwansdorf Camp. Parliamentary delegates came and went. She spent the occasional night at various transit camps as she visited the displaced persons at Millstadt, Bruch and Preffly. Lists were compiled of those who wished to emigrate and endless searches and documentation was undertaken to trace lost relatives. Violetta set herself the task of re-learning Russian but also found time to go boating and fishing at Spital. Her walks in the country invigorated her and she rejoiced to find 'whortleberries, strawberries, and mushrooms.' Her main base was at Scheifling still, and it was there that she learned of her brother Padge's death.

Near the end of April, after seeing a party of DP's leave Villack for Brazil, Violetta flew to England to visit the London School of Weaving, visit her publishers, but more importantly to spend some time consoling her nephew, JP, then just 23 years of age. In mid May she returned to Austria where she enigmatically reports 'no one to meet me' and Marem Camp 'a scene of desolation. Press deputation there, all very drunk.'

Once again great changes were to be made, and Violetta notes that ACA is taking over all UNRRA camps. Her job was due to end on July 1, with no further post fixed. Evidently she was offered a job at Leoben but turned it down for several unspecified reasons. At a cocktail party she learned that when one John Corsellis left on 5th July, she was to take over the Spital TB hospital. John, a young Quaker of 22, had directed the hospital and after he departed, he continued an interest in it.[3]

53

Violetta found her new post rather difficult. She appointed Sister Ella as her senior ward sister, and at her first staff meeting announced her intention to change the site of the hospital to Seebach. Sister Ella's appointment was not a success, and in the hot, thundery summer tensions were exacerbated, various incidents like a drunken soldier breaking in, and a revolver firing off added to the stress. Officials descended to query her decision to move the camp, there were delays with rations and upheavals in the kitchen. Colonel Grey left and was succeeded by Colonel Wade. After a quick flight to London for an operation on her teeth and a frantic reorganization of her house 'to be rented to the Wilsons', she returned to find the rumble of discontent still causing some problems. After an inspection 'where they seemed pleased' and the 'patients back now installed in new barracks' she held a small party and dance for everyone. Extracts from two letters give much insight into her feelings.

Violetta Thurstan, T.B. Hospital - Spittal am Drau, c/o M Assembly Camp, Civil Affairs (B.E.), B.T.A., C.M.F. 26 July 1947

Dear Mr. Corsellis, I expect you will be wondering how we are all getting on. Luckily we are doing well, all is quiet and harmonious - and everybody very good (except some naughty patients who went off to sleep in the camp for a change - coming back very early in the a.m. to their beds here). We are getting on quietly with some of the improvements. We have a recreation room now for the staff, and a flourishing occupational therapy room with a part-time teacher. It is still being proposed that we shall move to a better site - but nothing settled.

It has been a bad month for the patients, very hot and constant thunderstorms. We now have 84 patients - we get about 2 or 3 admissions every day.

I hope you are enjoying your much needed and deserved rest - I suppose the legal term does not begin till October? I am sure everybody would want to send you a message if they knew I was writing and then this letter would take many more pages than I have time for - so I had better stop. Yours sincerely, Violetta Thurstan

T.B. Hospital, c/o Civil Affairs (B.E.) Land Kaernten, B.T.A., C.M.F.,
26 November 1947

Dear Mr. Corsellis, I got your letter yesterday and as I happen to have a free moment (I don't get very many) I will answer your letter at once. First of all, we have moved. Away from the dust of the high road, the fog of the valley, the baking huts, the frightful difficulties with fuel, to a heavenly spot five minutes from a pine forest, beside a trout stream, glorious views of snow mountains, facing south and flooded with sunshine. It is an old Messerschmidt factory near Seeboden, Millstaedtersee - very well adapted for a hospital with central heating everywhere, a lovely kitchen all electric that can cook for 400 people, constant hot water, a very good recreation room for the patients with piano, radio - a carpenter's bench and other amenities, a separate chapel - a nice garden but not very big.

I found this place, and nagged at the authorities all the summer till at last I got permission to move. The day after I got permission, the agreement ACA and IRO (International Relief Organisation) was signed, and IRO at once sent a message to say we were not to move. I can't serve two masters, and as ACA had told me I could move, I went on quietly and got all the patients up here then there was a fine to do - people rushed down from Vienna, and Dr. C. said he did not approve of the move, as the place was too small - it was only a short term policy - it did not solve the T.B. problem, etc. etc. (Nobody ever thought it did). Dr. C. said he wanted a place for 1000 patients, we can only take 150 here. I left them all to squabble among themselves and went on with the move, and the comfort of having these patients so warm and happy and well done by - I can't describe.

IRO are very angry with me, but I can bear it - the patients are the important part. I could not leave them there to freeze. We were getting 1 metre of wood every 3rd day - only enough to heat the ward for an hour and a half in the evening - there was practically no wood in the camp. I had 106 patients and 37 out-patients waiting to come in, kitchen not big enough serving meals in relays till 8.30 pm, no laundry and with that large number of patients very very ill some of them, (one died the week before we came up) the washing had got quite beyond us.

L and the staff are very happy to be here and Dr. K. is beside himself with joy as he can really have his patients well looked after now. We are not being obstinate about it. If Dr. C. can find a place for 1000 patients, I shall be ready to move these people there. But there is no such building in all Austria as far as I know.

We are having the ambulance up here, and I hope a 15 CWT truck, so that we shall be fairly independent - rations come up in bulk. We have nothing to do now really with Spittal Camp. I wish you could pay us a little visit and see what a lovely place we have got. We are putting up 3 huts for the infectious cases - otherwise everyone is housed indoors.

You ask how I get on with Dr. K. Very well. I find him intelligent and cooperative. Old X is such a fool and started by being very uncooperative. So I had him in, and told him if he went on in that way, he would find himself standing on the road with his little bag waiting for a new job, and he has been much better since. But I don't find him very intelligent, and not at all up to date.

Y is moved to Salzburg. I have asked for a good welfare worker instead of a nurse, as I have a very good Oberschwester. No, I don't see much of Miss H. I am sure there is more news but I haven't more time so this will have to do to go on with. Very best wishes, Yours sincerely, Violetta Thurstan (4)

In 1966 she recalled some of those post-war experiences in her second novel, *The Foolish Virgin*. (5) The story concerns a young girl, Linda, recovering from an affair with a 'pro-Russian' who rejects the offer of a pampered holiday with an Aunt in Bermuda. She sees an advertisement to work in Austria and after citing her past hospital experience as a Red Cross driver, she is accepted to work with refugees in Vienna. Soon she is embroiled in the politics of the day. The camps mentioned in the book are those for displaced persons which Violetta would have visited, and the conditions experienced by Linda allow the reader an insight into Violetta's own perceptions. Her novel is set within a system where there are no automatic human rights, and Violetta uses it to applaud those unknown people who worked with compassion for the welfare of others.

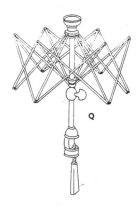

Chapter 9

Cornwall

After the Second World War, Violetta returned to the West Country to live. Though few details are extant related to how she spent her time in the late 1940s, it is known that her brother, Edward, died in 1947, followed by her nephew Richard in the same year. There had been three nephews, and now only Charles and John (JP) were alive. The latter, unmarried, was a frequent visitor to Violetta, in the school holidays away from his work at Swanbourne House School near Bletchley. Her house in Flushing was called Mary Mount, and he was there sufficiently often to make a circle of friends of his own, and to be appreciated by Violetta's friends for favours that he did for them all.

Violetta was a committed Catholic, and believed with fervour that she should set about to repair the lost Catholic connection between the English church and the 'Mother Church'. [1] Peter Matthewson, now a retired school teacher, and friend of Violetta, recalled one amusing anecdote related to her faith.

John Thurstan (JP) was very fond of Violetta. I was too, but he realized that she was a bit eccentric. Violetta was a convert to the Roman Catholic Church and, like all people of conviction, was keen to appear keen. So, when she lived at Flushing, she rigged up a little Chapel at Mary Mount and Canon X would cross the harbour from Falmouth on a Sunday morning to take Mass in her house for the eight or so Roman Catholics who gathered there.

JP, like myself, was a Church of England chap and he would warn me on a Saturday evening that we had to get out to Mylor for the 8 am service on the Sunday to be out of the way. One Sunday morning, we fled to Mylor Church in a great gale - most of the moored boats in Falmouth Harbour were floating just under the water. When he drove us back at about 8:30 or so, there was also a great storm of rain. We dashed from his car into Violetta's front door where we were confronted by this tiny indomitable, bent woman. "Come in, come in" she said. "If you belonged to the true church, you wouldn't have to get wet." She had a tremendously interesting character. (2)

As an early member of the Cornwall Guild of Weavers, Spinners and Dyers, Violetta had been co-opted onto the committee, which in 1951 met at the Bluebell Studio, St. Ives. In November of that year she was lecturing to the Guild at the Rose Vine Hotel, Portscatho on 'Ancient Textiles', illustrating her talk with examples, including several Coptic pieces and Braids from the Fayum, lent by the Victoria and Albert Museum.

In June of 1952, Violetta was in charge of the Guild stall at the Royal Cornwall Show. As a member of the selection committee she helped decide who could exhibit and sell. The International conference of Craftsmen in Pottery and Textiles was held in July at Dartington Hall, Devon, by courtesy of Leonard and Dorothy Elmhirst.(3) Robin Tanner, the educationalist who contributed much to the crafts, was invited to address the Conference. In his autobiography, *Double Harness*, he writes of, 'the galaxy of craftsmen that had come from all over the world to discuss their work and its place in modern society. Here was Hamada and Dr. Yanagi from Japan, Bernard Leach and Michael

Cardew, weavers from Scandinavia and England and men and women from industry and science.'[4] Violetta was a member of this august gathering. Shortly after, in October, she flew to the Scilly Isles to teach weaving to the children at the request of the Headmaster, Mr. McMillan Browse.

Violetta set up her own school of weaving in 1953. The advertisement for this venture read,

Miss Thurstan will be pleased to arrange instruction at the Mary Mount School of Weaving, St. Peter's Hill, Flushing. Students can be received for short or long courses covering all kinds of weaving and vat dyeing. Non resident students - single lesson 10/6d for 2 hours. Term of 16 lessons (32 hours) £6-16s-0d.

She was also organising sales and exhibitions at the Polytechnic Hall in Falmouth and selling her work in Newquay. An article on 'Peasant Art in Norway' published in 1954 [5], gives an interesting account of the Husfliederen or House of Peasant Art. this must have been a period of stability for Violetta as she continued to organise exhibitions and write articles and books throughout the 1950s.

Mrs. Rixon, a founder member of the Cornwall Guild of Weavers, Spinners and Dyers was elected as the first President in 1955, and Violetta became Vice President. Muriel Harvey, the Honorary Secretary of that time, who accompanied Violetta on some holidays, remembers her as a linguist. [6] When Mrs. Rixon resigned due to ill health in 1957, Violetta became President, a post which she held until her death in 1978.

A trip to Italy in 1955 provided Violetta with the stimulus for a lecture on the 'Tapestry and Handicrafts' of that country. Afterwards, another successful exhibition of work by Cornish Artists and Craftsmen was organised by her and officially opened by Mrs. Howard Spring.

Weaving without Tears was published in 1956, another busy year. An article on 'Teazles' appeared [7], and exhibitions and lectures continued, including one on 'Weaving in

Egypt'. Peter Collingwood [8] made his first visit to the Guild in that year and on his following visit in July, 1960 he stayed with Violetta.

An unusual appointment is noted in the Guild's news sheet No. 4 when it was stated that, 'It was agreed that Miss Thurstan carry on as Guild Delegate to the Cornwall Social Services Organisation.' No further details are given but the article also records that Miss Dorothy Wilkinson of the London School of Weaving held a one day school in the Social Services Centre in Truro.

Violetta wrote three articles for the *Weavers Journal*, the National Magazine of the Guilds, over an 18 month period. 'Dyeing in Ancient Times' deals with the history of dyes mainly in the middle and far east. [9] It includes a translation of a description of mordanting by the Roman Historian Pliny. Her second article [10] is concerned with blue dyes and the third [11], with red, crimson and scarlet. There is a reference to the wild madder plant (*rubia Peregrinia*) being found *'near the edges of woods in the West Country near the sea'*. When Mary Barker visited Cornwall to talk to the Guild in the '50s she recalls, 'I stayed with Violetta at her home in Flushing surrounded by her collection, delighting in her textile memories. There was time to take a walk to see where the wild madder plants grew.'[12]

As Secretary to the Catholic Women's League of Cornwall, she helped to organise the first party of Cornish Catholics to Rome since the Reformation. The President of the League was the Lady St. Levan, now the Dowager, who also accompanied the group with her husband, Lord St. Levan. Fortunately, Canon Bede Davis, now serving at St. Mary's Killigrew Street, Falmouth, had "not thrown away his diaries", and he had been a student at the English College in Rome when Violetta arrived with the Catholic Women's League on 2nd May 1958. He was sent to meet the party the following day and one of them was his mother.

The group stayed at the *Instituto S. Marta,* and later that afternoon twelve college students met up with Sir Marcus

Cheke, the British Minister, "to entertain the ladies there. At noon they had an audience with the Pope." A photograph taken on the roof of St. Peter's records the occasion, and Violetta is sitting in front holding their banner. On 16th May the following report was published in the *Western Morning News* ,

Cornish Catholic Women have audience with the Pope

Thirty three members of the Cornish Catholic Women's League, who have just returned from a pilgrimage to Rome, described yesterday the highlight of their trip - an audience with the Pope. With other groups of pilgrims they gathered for the audience at noon on a Sunday. The Pope was borne in on his chair preceded and followed by the Papal Guards. He gave an address in Italian followed by a little oration to each group. Turning towards the Cornwall Group he began "Dear Catholic pilgrims from Cornwall we bid you welcome to Rome" and ended by wishing a blessing on "all your dear ones at home".

With the group at the audience were the area chairman, Lady St. Levan, Miss Thurstan, M.M., the area secretary, the spiritual adviser Father Prior of St. Mary's Bodmin, Father Lawrence Byrne, and the chaplain, Canon Ford.

The pilgrims were shown famous churches and attended a garden party at the villa of the British Minister to the Holy See. The Minister, Sir Marcus Cheke and Lady Cheke, welcomed them all as they entered the lovely villa.

The Cornish group went also to Castel Gondolfo, the Pope's summer residence.

As an added highlight of the visit to Rome, a private audience was arranged with the Pope for the Lord and Lady St. Levan, the Minister and his wife, and Violetta.

Violetta's faith was very important to her, and her home continued to be open as a meeting place for services. In 1960 she was elected to a three year term as one of the Falmouth and Diocesan Presidents of the Catholic Women's League. [13]

61

In 1959, Violetta's article on 'Bedouin Life in the Egyptian Desert' was published. In the same year, Alice Hindson and Tadek Beutlich came to Cornwall to lecture on their respective specialisms, draw loom weaving and tapestry. Alice Hindson was one of the original '30s Guild to which Violetta had belonged.

Violetta remained a practising weaver. Two pictorial tapestries woven by her, one to celebrate the visit of King Olaf of Norway to the Regatta at Falmouth dated 1951, and the other a map of Cornwall, woven for the Cornwall Guild is dated 1954. The latter was exhibited in several places in Cornwall whenever the Guild held an event, and was exhibited in Chester at the Association of Guilds exhibition in 1960. At the Guild's October meeting in 1960, Violetta showed a sample of her work lent by Lord Methuen *'in which the quality of the indigo dyed wool had lost none of its richness in tone after twenty years in use as a rug.'* This piece must have been woven by Violetta just before the onset of the Second War.

An invitation to Guild members to attend an 'at home' at Flushing was sent in May, 1961. The next issue of the newsletter reported the visit and mentioned, 'Miss Thurstan was at home to members in her lovely house in Flushing'. On this occasion Violetta had apologised beforehand for not having any weaving of her own to show and asked members to take some of theirs. She did exhibit her own collection of rare textiles however, and continued to do this. In the August of 1962 there is mention of Spanish weaving. Much of her collection would have been acquired by Violetta herself but the authors believe, based on the variety known, that contributions also came from her family. There is no record of Violetta visiting the Congo or Peru but her brothers travelled extensively in the course of their careers. JP's father, Padge, had been the British Consul in Mexico and also in the Congo. There would have been ample opportunity for them to find relevant gifts for their sister.

The Society of Designer Craftsmen (formerly the Arts and Crafts Exhibition Society) held their 27th exhibition at Messrs. Arthur Sanderson and Sons Ltd., Berners Street, London W1 in November 1962. Violetta is listed as a full Craft Member although she was not exhibiting. Other weaving members included Mary Barker, Peter Collingwood, Ann Sutton, Tadek Beutlech, Hilda Breed and a fellow member of the Cornwall Guild, Joan Lee. Violetta had been a committee member of the Art & Craft Exhibition Society in 1938.

An ambitious exhibition, 'Weaving Today' was staged by the Guild at the County Museum, Truro, from June 28th to July 10th, 1965. The theme being 'Colours of Cornwall', guest exhibitors included Norah Biddulph (Bay), Peter Collingwood, Theo Moorman, The London School of Weaving and the Quantock Weavers. Since this was the first mention of Bay since the 1930s, perhaps the rift between them had healed. Violetta's collection of ancient textiles was also exhibited and there was a rota for stewarding. Violetta, now aged 86, elected to be at the Gallery every afternoon.

The Devon Guild of Craftsmen held their exhibitions annually in Torquay. The previous year's exhibitors had included such prestigious names as Marianne de Trey, Peter Collingwood, Peter Lanyon, Janet Leach and Theo Moorman. In 1965, Violetta reported on their current show,

The Devon Crafts Guild Exhibition, September 1965, Torre Abbey, Torquay.

The exhibition surpassed itself, especially in its lighting which was the best I have ever seen in such an exhibition, one middle light, each exhibit separately treated, a great stone jar 3 feet high, lighted by a cluster of pear shaped bulbs of different heights; a ridge of concealed ceiling lights making lights and shadows on a length of deep red silk, a table lamp on a sycamore table with handwoven mats and pale green pottery. Everything was arranged in a series of little rooms; the hardboard partitions being of neutral colour did not detract from the exhibits. Mrs. Bosence sent some lovely wool but there was not as much weaving as in other years...my little piece was well hung. There was some well executed embroidery too and I wished as I so often do that we included embroidery with our weaving, in ancient times there was no distinction made between them, weaving looked like embroidery and embroidery looked like weaving....[14]

In the Guild's November 1965 address list, Violetta is recorded, for the last time, as living at Mary Mount, Flushing. A new address appears in an invitation in June 1966, where Kathleen Defee's name also appears for the first time. Kathleen Innes Whittington Defee, formerly an almoner at Guys Hospital, London, had been widowed. It was suggested that Kathleen should come to Cornwall as a companion/housekeeper to Violetta, who was little interested in home comforts. The idea was agreeable to them both and the initially casual arrangement developed into a friendship that lasted to Violetta's death. Sometimes Violetta was indifferent to Kathleen's stable support, and friends and relatives can recall occasions when Kathleen was treated brusquely when certain important visitors attended meetings at home. Kathleen was likely to be publically admonished for some trivial omission or commission, but nevertheless, the two women remained firm companions.

Kathleen managed the accounts, cooked, cleaned, drove and supported Violetta with her voluminous correspondence and travels. She became a friend to Violetta's relatives who appreciated her kindness, and was relied upon to welcome visitors, expected or otherwise, with an affectionate hint as to Violetta's current state of health. Violetta was, therefore, free to pursue her interests.

The Weaving Exhibition at Penryn - Report by the Secretary

The annual exhibition this year was held at Penryn in the Old Mill House. For a little while it seemed as if no exhibition would be possible this year and then our President offered to lend us her charming drawing room for a whole week and we were only too delighted to accept. I am sure that all who went to Penryn will agree that our work looked very colourful set off by Miss Thurstan's white walls and that the actual receipts were helped enormously by her enthusiastic salesmanship. Members are to be congratulated on the admirable way they arrived on time to take their turn of duty and we must all be pleased with the result. A very special thank you must be said to Mrs. Defee who so effortlessly plied everyone with coffee or tea all day long and there is no doubt that those 'cuppas' helped several would-be purchasers to come to a decision. We must also thank Mr. J. Thurstan for help in a hundred ways during the week. The Guild benefited so greatly by the kindness of the family at the Old Mill House that it seemed only fitting to offer two bottles of sherry as a very small token of our thanks.[15]

In 1966, Violetta's novel, *The Foolish Virgin*, was published. Margery Hicks, writing in the *Cornish Review*, No. 2 that year, about 'Weaving in Cornwall' devoted a paragraph to Violetta and her achievements, ending with, 'this tiny, apparently fragile, indomitable woman is at present in Greece advising on the revival of weaving in the impoverished district of Euoboea.' Ann Pike, a friend of Violetta, recalls that this visit was made at the request of Noel Baker, and that Violetta was 88 years old at the time. Hilda Breed [16] recorded that Dorothy Wilkinson at the age of 82 also went to Greece that year at the invitation of Barbara and Francis Noel Baker, who were running a cottage industry in North Euoboea. Presumably, these two indomitable ladies, who had shared so many weaving experiences, were there together.

Two eminent speakers came as visiting lecturers to the Guild in 1966, Marianne Straub whose subject was 'A Handweaver in Industry' and Robert Patterson, from the folk museum in York who spoke on 'The Story of Wool'. Violetta, as President, introduced them and summarised Patterson's lecture,

Guild Members will remember that in Dr. Patterson's recent lecture in Truro he mentioned that the red obtained from Kermes was one of the most beautiful and permanent of dyes. Kermes are the dried bodies of tiny insects found in the red berries of the Holly oak. The dye is prepared in the same way as cochineal which it much resembles and produces shades of red, scarlet, crimson and rose. This oak is not found in the British Isles and is difficult to obtain. It is plentiful in Eastern Europe especially in the mountain districts of Euobea in Greece. The dye was formerly used for the scarlet of soldiers' uniforms. [17]

On November 19th, 1966, the inaugural meeting of the World Craft Council - British Section was held in London, and Violetta was invited to attend. She reported that, 'The purpose of the Council shall be to provide services to craftsmen around the world. Such services will include, among other things, providing a clearing house for creative, technical, economic and social exchanges and a focus of co-operation between craftsmen.' [18] She attended a further meeting held at the Victoria and Albert Museum and spoke of her concerns for remote counties such as Cornwall. Her report back to the Guild [19] included the following remarks,

There were 450 people odd, at the meeting of the World Crafts Council at the V&A Museum on March 18th, 1967, very interesting people too: The Chair, Mr. Pope-Hennessy, the Museum Director; the Director of UNESCO who had flown in from New York specially for the meeting; the American Director of the Council; the organising secretary for the British section, Henry Rothschild of Primavera. Nearly all crafts were represented, the potters in the majority; Bernard Leach spoke and I sat next to David Leach....There were a lot of weavers and Ann Sutton spoke on the way weavers could maintain themselves by weaving. Mr. Pope Hennessy said that not nearly enough importance was placed on the crafts in Great Britain and he proposed to help rectify this by holding a Crafts Exhibition in the Museum at least every two years.

During the afternoon, I asked the Council to realise that not all craftsmen lived within a bus ride of London, and what did the Council propose to do for people who lived in remote places such as Cornwall? I asked how they could expect the high standard of work that the speakers were advocating when we had no Crafts Centre and speakers passed us by. I told them that the Cornwall Guild of Weavers had requested the Municipal Council in Truro to provide for a Crafts Centre in its new development plan, but the City Fathers had rejected the idea.

When I sat down, others got up who claimed that they too lived in remote places - Northumberland, West Wales, etc. and the Chairman asked Mr. Rothschild to answer. "The Council," he said "had sympathy will all I said and it proposed to help by visiting, giving advice, talks, organising exhibitions, anything we liked, but we must write and ask him what we wanted as no one could know our needs if we did not voice them. He hoped we WOULD write and ask for help but we should have to provide a hall, an audience and so on."

Violetta did not pass up the opportunity to follow up on Mr. Rothschild's offer, and the Weaving Guild was instrumental in inviting him to visit Cornwall. And similarly, it was probably not coincidence, that soon after the meeting a coach trip was arranged for the Cornish Guild to visit the pottery of David Leach at Bovey Tracey where a pottery demonstration and a talk about the World Crafts Council were included.

In November of 1967 Henry Rothschild visited Cornwall at the invitation of the Guild of Weavers and the meeting was thrown open to all craftspeople in Cornwall as well as to the general public. The meeting place was the new Chapter House in Truro Cathedral, the perfect venue for such a meeting being a work of excellent craftmanship in wood, stone, glass and concrete. The meeting was well attended with about 200 people. Following this, discussions began at the end of 1967 concerning the formation of the Cornwall Craft Guild. Violetta recorded that, 'Our Guild, as the only organised body of craftsmen in the county, is now being expected to instigate the necessary steps towards forming such a body."[20]

Joan Lee, then Head of the Department of Fashion and Design at the Plymouth School of Art, and a member of the Guild, attended the Annual 1968 conference of the World Crafts Council in Peru. She then was instrumental in founding the Cornwall Crafts Association in 1973, with a number of others. By this time, Violetta was well into her nineties, but at least she had started the ball rolling.

p. 68 *The visit to Rome by the Cornish Catholic Women's League, Western Morning News photo, May 16, 1958.*

p. 68 *Violetta in March, 1972 at Urchfont Manor with Hetty Wickens and Isabel McGraghan. Photo by Mary Powell.*

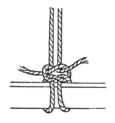

Chapter 10

'her indomitable spirit'

Violetta gave a talk on tapestry weaving to the Guild in January of 1968. Peter Collingwood visited again in February. The July sale of work was again held at the Old Mill House, and in the month before that, Violetta went to speak to the London Guild about Peruvian Tapestries; her old acquaintance, Dorothy Wilkinson, spoke to the Guild in November, and her talk on linen weaving was illustrated by a selection from Violetta's collection of textiles.

Violetta's Christmas message to the Guild, in her 90th year, read:

If you have any space in the newsletter I should love to send the Guild a message to give them my love and wishes for a very happy Christmas and all that is good in 1969 in spite of austerities - which I suppose we ought to take as a challenge. [1]

A Crafts Council exhibition in the early part of 1969, was a travelling exhibit showing the best of British Crafts, with sections set aside at each venue for invited local craftsmen. The exhibition was staged at the Plymouth City Art Gallery, and Violetta was one of the six local members to exhibit. Margery Hicks reported that,

' The rugs, three by Violetta Thurstan, would have shown better could they have been flat under some pottery and furniture perhaps. Our President's were in tapestry weave, one in the natural greys and black of Australian fleece and another, my favourite, a gentle blue, patterned by small oblongs of varying colours.' [2]

Throughout the next years Violetta continued to attend and chair meetings, sometimes acting as a fall-back speaker when others were unable. In her Presidential letter of 1971, Violetta is optimistic,

Very dear Members,

First I must send my best wishes for a Happy New Year and all that is good to everyone. I am proud indeed to be your president. We begin the new year with a new home. We had to give up our dear old British Legion Hall where we all met so often, and went through a difficult period before finding another suitable home. Now we have a splendid one in the new Village Hall at Carnon Downs where we held such a successful exhibition last summer; it has every possible convenience including a big car park. We shall have to live up to the standard of our new home, ever striving for higher ideals and more beautiful work matching the best traditions of the past with the new techniques, new tools, new materials of the future. So I wish you Happy Days. Violetta Thurstan [3]

Links with the Crafts Council continued through 1971. Joan Lee gave an account of the World Crafts Council conference in Peru and in Ireland to the Guild and Cyril Wood, Director of the Crafts Council of Great Britain spoke at an open meeting. In June, Dorothy Wilkinson was seriously ill and unable to give her promised talk. Once again Violetta stepped into the breach with a talk on 'Vegetable Dyes'. In October, the Reverend and Mrs. Lavery, members of the Guild, invited her to talk on the History of Textiles in St. John's Hall, Truro. At the same time, an article by Violetta was published in the *Journal of the Guild of Weavers, Spinners and Dyers* [4]. It was entitled 'Mortlake, A Hundred Years of Tapestry' and traced the history of the Mortlake Factory founded by James I to its demise in 1773. The article, an edited version of a chapter in her book, *A Short History of Decorative Textiles*, is illustrated with a photograph, 'Venus and Adonis watch Atlanta and Hippomenes as lions' provided by courtesy of the V&A.

Hetty Wickens, author of *Natural Dyes for Spinners and Weavers*, attended a dyeing course in March, 1972 at Urchfont Manor, Wiltshire, at which Violetta was tutor. There were 35 students, and the enthusiasm lasted every evening until the small hours of the morning. Hetty recalled,

' We all enjoyed meeting someone whose books were so well known to us. There is one part of her talk which I always remember with a smile and have often repeated. When asked about the use of bilberries as a dye, Violetta Thurstan's reply was, "Yes they make a good colour if you can bear not to make them into a pie." [5]

Violetta spoke to the Guild in February, 1974 on 'Weaving in Roumania' but missed the Annual General Meeting in March. This was, of course, most unusual, and the Newsletter report stated: ' Knowing Miss Thurstan as we do, we are confident that her indomitable spirit will triumph over a distressing - but as we hope temporary - eye condition, and that she will soon be with us again in person as well as in spirit.' [6]

The June newsletter confirmed their confidence. ' It was splendid to have Miss Thurstan among us at the April meeting. In May she is off to Yugoslavia conducting one of her famous and enviable tours;....We all hope that one day a biographer will record the life of this Woman for All Seasons whose frail appearance utterly belies her indomitable spirit.' [7]

Violetta's message to the Guild at Christmas that year was simple,

71

This year the Guild is celebrating its 22nd Christmas and I am wishing all members a very happy Christmas despite all the difficulties prophesied for 1975. I hope it will be a happy and prosperous year. Difficulties are a challenge and so I hope for an even higher standard of work and a greater measure of success to you all. Many good wishes from your President. [8]

Her message to the guild in 1976 was still concerned about gloomy forecasts,

Very Dear Members, This is a word to wish you all a happy and successful New Year. We have been promised plenty of difficulties in 1976 but I wish you all courage and a joyful spirit in surmounting them. With my love. [9]

The Chairman, Veronica Hudd, wrote in the March newsletter of that year, 'It was lovely to have our President at the A.G.M. she is a real tonic and a wonderful person.' The secretary, Britt Varcoe, outlined, '...plans in the pipeline, such as a Dyers' Garden for Cornwall, where our famous President is going to help with her vast knowledge'. The Dyers Garden was to be at the Probus Demonstration Gardens north of Truro, where the Guild was also to establish their new meeting place. The Garden was subsequently named the Violetta Thurstan Dye Garden and remains to this day.

A letter from Violetta to Anne Pike on March 2nd, 1976, gives an account of the visit of Peter Blake, the Probus Garden administrator, asking for her advice on dye plants. The same letter records a visit to St. Austell with Kathleen to hear Mrs. Thatcher speak to the Conservative Association. Violetta also held appointment as the President of the Penryn Conservatives at that time.

When Westward Television planned a series of six programmes entitled 'Which Craft' Sheila Brough was invited to act as Adviser. The first programme of the television series dealt with weaving, spinning and dyeing, and Violetta made a guest appearance. [10] Sheila had interviewed Violetta in 1976, and written an article about her for *Cornish*

Life magazine. An excerpt from this article, entitled 'A Travellers Tale' [11] gives us a picture of Violetta amongst her memorabilia.

Today Violetta Thurston, a diminutive silver-haired figure, lives quietly in a tranquil 18th century house in Penryn. She does not care to reveal her age, but we were astonished by her vitality and constant joy in her garden, and in the many treasures she has acquired over the years. The house is a delight to the eye - there are ancient pottery toy animals from the Bedouin village, a linen shroud from Luxor dating from 2,000 BC, an exquisite cloth of gold embroidery on cream muslin from Bengal. From Russia a woven sash with the Lord's Prayer inscribed in old Slavonian characters, worn by soldiers going to the front; from Crete a display of ancient pottery; an example of Coptic weaving from 400 AD; fine embroidered silks from Persia. On the floor are the handwoven carpets of the Bedouins combining sheeps wool and camel hair, unusual, as Violetta points out because the warp shows on the upper side. In the dining room hangs one of Violetta's own works. On the well-polished dresser there is a fine collection of Dresden and old English china. From the walls the ancestors look down, handsome upright gentlemen in naval uniforms, medals shining, braids gleaming, their wives and daughters demure in sprigged muslins, reminiscent of Jane Austin's country families.

Five days after her 97th birthday in 1977, Violetta gave what was to be her last talk to the Guild on 'My Life Among the Bedouins'. In May, Peter Collingwood visited Cornwall and admired the Guild's gift of the Cornish Tapestry to Truro Cathedral. Violetta, being in Yugoslavia, had delegated her responsibilities to the Vice-president.

The Cornwall Crafts Association made Violetta an Honorary Life Member with the following citation, inscribed on vellum by calligrapher Wendy Gould of Cubert. At the time of the presentation ceremony, Violetta was not well, and Britt Varcoe took the certificate to her at Penryn.

CORNWALL CRAFTS ASSOCIATION
wish to record that the gift of
HONORARY LIFE MEMBERSHIP
has been made to
VIOLETTA THURSTAN
in recognition of her
DISTINGUISHED SERVICE TO THE CRAFTS

An article by Brian Wall about Violetta in *The Packet* newspaper [12] described her as 'a tornado of immense energies, self effacing, demure, charmingly courteous and above all endowed with that sort of courage that has throughout our history made roaring lions out of gentle lambs.' The article was being published in connection with the planned publication of her last book, *The Hounds of War Unleashed.* [13]

Violetta was warmly welcomed at the Guild's Annual General Meeting in March, 1978, with the comment that she approved of the new premises. This may have been her first visit to the Probus Gardens.

A month later on April 13th, 1978, Violetta Thurstan died. Kathleen and JP were both with her.

In Violetta's Will, she left 100 pounds for the use of 'the little Catholic Church at Penryn' and also requested a Requiem Mass so that 'she should be buried with the full Rites of the Holy Catholic Church.' At her death all of Violetta's requests were honoured, and the Service of Burial was taken by the Reverend Michael Lock. Her nine military medals were buried with her.

Her obituary in the Guild's Newsletter and subsequently in the *Weavers Journal*, was written by Margery Hicks.[14] Its final paragraph concluded,

' Her fragile appearance masked an indomitable spirit: she had the heart of a lion, the mind of a scholar, the enthusiasm of a child. Perhaps it was this last that so endeared her to us for, in spite of the growing disabilities of age to which she gallantly refused submission nor ever referred, she shared actively in every interest of the Guild and was never failing in zest and encouragement. In this, and in the lustre lent by her name, she must be irreplaceable. We acknowledge with deep gratitude the debt we owe her and we salute her memory.'

***

Not many people remain who knew Violetta well, those who do reveal a many-faceted being: a respected textile expert, knowledgeable courier, devout Catholic, eccentric Aunt, mischievous companion, efficient organiser, brilliant lecturer, competent linguist and compassionate carer. During our research many anecdotes were shared with us. They did not all fit into the main text of the monograph but we believe that they illustrate other aspects of Violetta's many relationships and are worth recording. The names of the contributors of the following anecdotes are included in the footnotes for this chapter.[15]

She kept a sharp eye on her workers both for quality and slackness. They needed both close supervision and encouragement but she also had compassion for their poverty and their ills caused by a low diet. One wonders what became of the Bedouins and their workshops while the desert war raged round them. (MB)

In the early forties, Violetta had somehow discovered my textile training. One evening when I came back from shore leave she was waiting for me (with her dog) to show me some samples and weaving photos, talking so enthusiastically with no heed of time, that I got a black mark for being late back to my cabin. (MB)

When in Rumania she was able to translate an ancient Slavonic manuscript, to the delight of the custodian who

75

left everyone else standing and excorted her personally round the museum. (anon)

When Violetta's Father returned to England, he lived with his sister Louise. A table which is a family heirloom was traditionally passed to the eldest daughter. Aunt Louise refused to pass this to Violetta (the rightful heir) as she had become a Roman Catholic. (CT)

I met her through the church at Flushing. She wrote an extremely well-written book on refugees - she was a ball of fire. I followed her through as Chair of the Catholic Women's League at the end of her three year term. I fell into it. "You don't have to do anything except go to Exeter twice a year and take a meeting down here." What happened? There were thirteen places to visit and twice-yearly meetings. "Lovely to be involved," she said. (MM)

Wanting a speaker I consulted her. I introduced one doctor as a family advice consultant--who said "Oh no, I'm here to talk about contraception" and this to Catholics! Violetta told me afterwards, "so good for us". (MM)

She was not easy to have as a friend. She was so definite you see, but she was very kind and we got on well. We met over Russia and had a link there--the trip to Rome went beautifully. If she said it would be - it was--but she did keep disappearing- to some other interest perhaps. (DLSL)

She never talked about her nursing training. She was the kindest and loveliest of people. We had hilarious times with her. During the Russian campaign her fiancee was killed. That was a great sorrow to her.(Kay urged her to write the *Hounds of War Unleashed*).(AP)

She insisted on doing everything herself. Everything was so well-organised, it was a joy to go on holiday with her. (AP)

No dates of course - she was a devil for dates - would never let Kay or I have her passport. She never wanted us to know how old she was. (AP)

Violetta boasted to me that she had never boiled an egg. (SB)

[How does this correspond with her excellent examination results in 'sickroom cookery'. See page 9. Ed.]

She took parties of women - went out and tried it first. We never stayed anywhere with more than two hotels. We really got to know the country. (AP)

I remember once Kay and I drove Violetta out for a picnic near Cadgwith. We parked fairly near and spread the rugs and got out the picnic. We had been so careful---we went back to the car and she was gone. There she was, she had climbed up some rocks. Poor Kay, she was not very good on rocks. I was a bit cross, but we packed up and joined her on top of a rock balanced on the edge. (VT was then in her nineties.Ed.) (LT)

She once said "Whatever things I've done, I would have wished to be a writer." (LT)

She was always planning something else. She couldn't rest. Yes, she's done so much. She would occasionally tell you of her ventures. (LT)

We went to Roumania on one of Violetta's marvellous trips. She wore a wig belonging to one of the party and every day chopped off some strands so that it got quite bald. When we crossed the frontier she flung it gaily out of the train. (AP)

My husband didn't like her at first but afterwards admired her enormously. (LT)

Kay (Kathleen) wouldn't live in Flushing so they moved. In Flushing the staircase was precipitous and the carpet never fitted. (AP)

Very successful trip to Yugoslavia - someone said 'Miss T has picked ANOTHER winner. It is a delightful and interesting place. Super hotel and a free bus to a beach with miles of sand. [postcard from K. Defee to AP)

She sat in a corner at meetings (of the Cornwall Guild) and said very little, but she always wore a hat with a turned down brim. (MV)

She had two hats, one for summer with flowers on, and a plain one for winter. (WSG)

I knew she sent all her information up to a television company. They lost the script. What a pity. We wanted to do 'This is your life' but most had died. (MT)

She was a very private person in many ways. She did not seem to have been a happy person. (LT)

I went to Majorca with Kay and Violetta and JP - who was so nice with the old people. (AP)

In her last years I would go to see her most weekends and attempted to sing to her. (LT)

So many little things you cannot put into a book. (VT)

Her family remember her as Auntie Vi---She was simply marvellous fun. (MT)

Violetta remained intellectually alert to her death in 1978. JP and Kathleen were the executors of her Will. John was given all the royalties from her books, and both executors were empowered to dispose of all assets as they felt appropriate in order to generate a life-time income for Kathleen. On the latter's death, everything reverted to John, who then sold the house. On his death in 1987, he made his legatees the remaining members of his family and his old college, Magdalene College, Cambridge.

Violetta's knowledge of the nuances of different cultures together with her experience of ninety-nine years of living from the nineteenth century security of Victorian England to the confused global recession of the twentieth century made meeting her an unforgettable experience, and highlight for many. She triumphed over ill health, discouragement and loss but with stubborn ambition used her talents and opportunities to maximum effect.

Everyone that the present authors have met recounted incidents with vividness and happy confidence. Rather than a sense of loss, all reflected a shared and consistent level of respect and affection for Violetta. But, we discovered that living with these memories for 18 months was less simple. It is easy to look back over this period and arrive at a fairly plausible assessment of Violetta's achievements. It has been a significant, even poignant, experience, to wander through her life and to study accounts of particular historical events as seen by one very individual woman. So, many thanks, Violetta ---a celebration indeed!

p. 80 *Violetta outside Old Mill House, Penryn, in her nineties. Photo by Robert Roskrow.*

Appendices

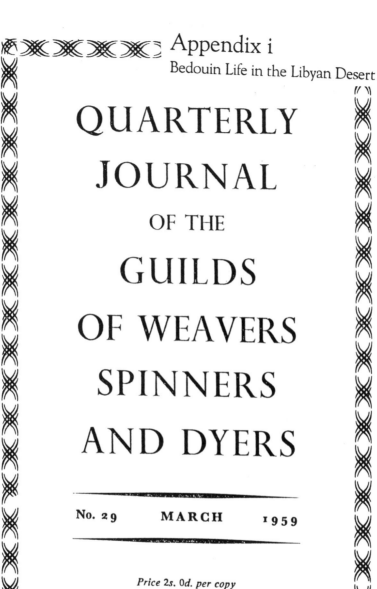

QUARTERLY

JOURNAL

OF THE

GUILDS

OF WEAVERS

SPINNERS

AND DYERS

No. 29   MARCH   1959

Price 2s. 0d. per copy

Bedouin Life in the Libyan Desert

*Reminiscences of her work as a Director of Crafts in the early
nineteen-twenties*

By VIOLETTA THURSTAN

TURN your backs on the shops, the crowds and the hotels of
Alexandria, and take the coast road westwards to the Salt
Lake. Cross three causeways, sparkling white and encrusted
with salt, and you are on the fringe of the great Western Desert which
stretches for hundreds of miles till it finally merges into the Sahara.
If you went far enough in the right direction, you would find our camp
at Burg el Arab. This village is not far from El Alamein, and the soldiers
who fought here in the last war know this road well enough. But in the
years before the war, this desert road was a lonely sandy track, where
you were unlikely to meet anyone but a nomad Bedouin with his
camel, a shepherd muffled up to the eyes in his white cloak, leading
his flock of goats and sheep, or an occasional cluster of Bedouin tents
round a well.

The village of Burg el Arab lies on the only ridge of high land running parallel with the coast. Some little way from the village was the
camp, of half a thousand Bedouins living in the same kind of black
goats' hair tents that were used in the time of Abraham. 'Tents', you
would call them, but the Bedouin always talks about his 'house',
whether it is the spacious tent of a sheikh, or one smaller than a Boy
Scout's tent in which, if the owner laid himself out straight at night,
his head and feet would stick out at either end. It is in fact his house, his
portable home, and he can pack it up with all his belongings and be
off in less than twenty minutes. If a bad dust-storm or heavy rain comes
on, his womenfolk will take it down and put it up again with the
opening turned away from the weather. There is no rent to pay, no
house shortage, and the desert is wide enough for all to live in it who
wish to do so.

The weaving of the tent is women's work; any dirty or disagreeable
work is women's work. There is no machinery, not even a spinning
wheel, so they sit patiently on the ground spinning the smelly un-
washed goats' hair on their home-made wooden spindles. The thread is
held between their great toe and their second toe and is skilfully spun
into yarn by a very light movement of the hand. When they have
enough, they wind it into balls and it is ready for weaving. There are
no looms. The length of material required is measured out on the
sand, the weaver sits on the ground and a little girl runs up and down
with the big ball of wool, paying it out as she goes. As she approaches
the weaver, the latter takes a loop of wool and winds it crossways on
two sticks to make the shed. This process goes on till the whole warp is
spread out lengthways on the sand. There is no reed; the strands of
wool are too close and thick for that. The ends of wool nearest the
woman are now secured to another stick and weighted down with stones.

The weaving of the strips for the tent now begins. A long wooden

6

sword round which the weft is wound serves as a shuttle; the weaver picks up the alternate warp threads incredibly quickly with her fingers, pushes through the sword and then picks the weft down with a gazelle horn till the material is close and strong and practically rain-proof. Tent pieces are sometimes plain but often ornamented with horizontal stripes in natural colours. When enough strips have been woven, they are sewn together. Sewing, being a clean and easy job, is of course men's work.

Carpets and rugs are made by the same method but they are made in the Government workshop, and the Bedouins are paid for their work according to their skill. Warp spinners are paid rather more than weft spinners and are slightly higher in the social scale. Weavers are in a higher social class still.

Before the war, you could see the towers and gates of the workshops for many a mile round. They were built by the Egyptian Government out of the chiselled stones that the Romans left behind sixteen centuries before. The camp is pitched on the site of an early Christian settlement. There are tombs nearby and a few heaps of stones that were once ancient Christian churches before Mahomed thundered through the desert with fire and sword, razing them all to the ground. The ground round the camp is littered with broken Roman glass, shards of pottery and occasional old coins.

The Bedouin tents are clustered round the workshops. On the outskirts our shepherds live in their tents with the goats and sheep around them. They only partially supply our need for wool. We need a great deal, for we make more than 2,000 carpets and rugs in the year.

Many of the Bedouin sheikhs in the desert own large flocks of sheep and goats which exist on the coarse dry scrub growing in the sand and among the rocks near the coast, as long as there is any. In the scorching summer, when there is no vegetation at all, they receive a little 'Tibn' (chopped barley straw) so that it can be imagined that they are in pretty poor condition by the time the next rains are due. Inland, there is no vegetation, no water, except in a few oases, and the desert is empty of all but sand.

Prosperity depends entirely on the rainfall. About Christmas time you will see the Bedouins looking anxiously into the sky for clouds and earnestly discussing the prospects of rain. Some very good showers in January and the desert, as if by a miracle, springs up into green herbage. Charming desert flowers appear, tiny stocks, about 1½ inches high with an intoxicatingly sweet scent, narcissus that the Romans planted with bulbs brought from home hundreds of years before, clusters of tall pink asphodels, yellow daisies and scarlet poppies.

By the middle of March all is gone and the long scorching summer sets in. March is the month when the shearing begins. If there has been a fair amount of rain, the sheep have put on weight and the wool is at its best. The quality of desert wool, however, is always dry and hard, suitable for making nearly indestructible carpets, but quite unsuitable for dress materials.

7

As we have never enough wool ourselves for all our needs, we go out to the native suks or markets to buy as many fleeces as possible. One has to be wide awake on these occasions, for the children of the desert, full of guile, are not at all above dipping the fleeces in camel's milk and rubbing them in the sand to increase their weight, or tying two or three fleeces together with large stones in their interior. The bales are packed on the backs of camels which make their slow way to the workshops where the wool is unpacked, washed, carded, spun, dyed, and finally woven into beautiful carpets and rugs.

Before the war, the Egyptian Government was responsible for the Bedouin industries and the rugs, kelims, and khoorgs (saddle bags) went to the agents in Cairo, Port Said, Luxor and Jerusalem to be sold. As far as possible, the old traditional patterns are adhered to, amplified and developed here and there, but always on Bedouin lines. At sunrise all are astir and when the big bell begins to ring, little groups of Bedouins enter the gates. The whole family arrives, including the newest-born baby who is slung on his mother's back as she works. The black tents are deserted for the day.

My first duty is to go round the workshops. I see that the spinners have enough wool for the day's work. I speak to every weaver—there are over two hundred of them—and inspect their work. They are squatting on the carpet they are making, the length of the warp pegged out on the sand, travelling up it as they work. Sometimes they are making a special order, and then a careful measurement is necessary, for a few inches either way means very little to a Bedouin. Then comes a long discussion with the Bedouin forewoman, as to what carpets should be made for stock. The finishing and sewing are done by the old men and enough time has to be allowed to look at their work and crack a joke with them before going on to the dyehouse.

As you approach this, you become aware of a most terrible smell; that is why the dyehouse is some way up among the rocks above the camp—a scorching climb in hot weather. The smell is due to the indigo pit dug deep in the ground. The indigo has to ferment or get 'ripe' before the glorious deep sapphire blue colour can be extracted. After a batch (about 100 lbs.) of wool has been dyed, the pit has to 'rest' for a week, then new ingredients are put in (but the old ingredients are never cleared out) and when the pit is 'ripe', which takes another week, the new batch is dyed.

Many of our dye plants are found close at hand. The bulbs of the beautiful tall asphodel crowned with branches of pale pink flowers give a very permanent pinky-fawn colour. Tamarisk bushes that grow near the Salt Lake yield a beautiful green; the wild mignonette (weld) that springs up among the rocks on the coast in February yields a fine yellow. No chemical or artificial dyes are allowed to be used: pure plant dyes only. Fine ranges of colour from pure white to fawn yellow and from pale tea colour to deep brown are obtained from different shades of sheep and goats' wool. The practice of seeing everything in terms of carpets grows on one and I can hardly ever see a camel or a goat of an

8

unusual colour without at once wanting to steal up and shear him. Baby camels in particular have silky delicious hair of pale yellow or dove grey.

After this exhausting process is over, for the indigo is indeed sometimes *very* 'ripe', I have to repair to the office. Here the Bedouin forewoman awaits me, with my clerk, two Bedouins with the weighing machine and two more who bring in the carpets finished the day before and who stay to see the fun. This is 'inspection of carpets'. At one time the Bedouins were paid so much a carpet and then, human nature being what it is, they made as many as possible as fast as possible. The result was careless mistakes in the pattern, knots, bad edges and loose weaving, which made the carpet quite unsaleable. This would not do, so I decreed that they must be paid by the day. This was fine for them, for they got paid the same, however little they did, and they just curled themselves up on their carpet and had a siesta whenever they felt like it.

I had to put my brains to work to circumvent this and at last I got an inspiration. The forewoman would lay the carpet out before me. I would inspect it carefully, pronounce the quality to be A or B or C. A carpet with beautiful weaving and colouring, above the average, was an A carpet, and carried a special wage. The ordinary carpets of a standard of weaving which everybody was expected to reach, was a B carpet, and the worker received the ordinary standard wage. If I pronounced a carpet to be of C quality, the forewoman threw it contemptuously into a corner. The Bedouins watching, hawked and spat, and crackling with laughter, went out to tell the unfortunate of her carpet's fate. She received only the lowest wage it was possible to give.

By this time, it was midday, and in the hot weather I was pretty well all in. I went off to wash and change before lunch. 'Change' meant taking off every garment and putting on clean ones, especially during the 'flea season', March to July. The Bedouins had two proverbs, 'The king of the fleas lives here'. I am sure that was true. The other was 'The fleas go away when the dates get ripe', and it was true that after July, life was not quite so intolerable.

After lunch, back to the office. The carpets have to be weighed and the weight, price, worker's name and other details entered in the register by the clerk. The packers and sewers are now called in, then the forewoman returns to her work in the workshops, the finished bales are sewn up and put in the mule cart, ready to be sent off to the agents.

Then comes a visit to the dispensary. In summer especially, when there is very little milk, the toddlers get a small supply of tinned milk which, being of the sweetened variety, they love, or someone comes along with a bad cough and wants some cough mixture, or someone else had a bad cut which has gone septic. On the whole, they heal quickly and well, but in the long Ramadan fast, or in the hot weather if there has been very little winter rain, they begin to go down like ninepins. We have no doctor here. There is a desert hospital with a doctor, but it is a long way off and the Bedouins resist, with all the

9

energy they have, any attempt to send them there. During an epidemic of smallpox, an Egyptian doctor was sent out here, armed with a supply of vaccine, to vaccinate everyone. A great many ran away and stayed away till he had gone. Everybody hotly denied that he even knew of the existence of a sick person. Going into one of the tents, the doctor saw the lid of a wooden chest move, and looked inside to find a woman covered with smallpox pustules. Granny was too ill to move away with the rest of the family, so they stuffed her in the chest and shut the lid until such time that the doctor had gone.

Now it is four o'clock, the bell rings and the day's work is done. I often stand by the gate saying goodnight to the workers as they stream back to their tents to prepare the evening meal. This is the best time to see the camp, for in the sunset the tents stand out black against a sky of flame and rose and gold, and there are blue wreaths of smoke curling up from the little fire of thorns or desert scrub in front of each tent. Near the door of the tent sit the menfolk; in the background, the women are preparing supper. In good times there will be plenty of rice, onions, barley cakes, perhaps camel's milk cheese, and sweet weak tea. Hospitality to guests is the first law of the desert, and the people will gladly share their meal with any passing stranger.

In the evening, if it is a feast day, they may dance in the firelight, but more often, they will talk. There is plenty to talk about. The rain or absence of rain, a desert feud, blood money, the barley tax or any other such iniquity of the Government, a marriage or a death—any of these will afford an inexhaustible topic of conversation. Then one by one, the flickering fires go out and the dogs stop howling. But the beauty of the starlight night, the wide spaces and the silences of the desert remains.

———

Appendix ii

Chronology, World War II Service Records, and List of Medals

VIOLETTA THURSTAN 1879-1978
CHRONOLOGY

Age	Date	Event
	1879	Birth, 4 February, Hastings, Sussex Anna Violet Thurstan (Violetta) Brothers born - Edward (1880) Norman (1889) & Denzil (1889)
12	1888	Family living in Canary Isles
	1891	To school in Germany
20	1898	Working in Wibney (sic)
	1899	To East London Hospital
	1900	Living in Taunton. Joins London Hospital as a probationer
	1905	Qualifies as a nurse, 11 March
31	1907	Returns to Bristol
	1910	In London
	1911	In Leeds. Nephew Charles born.
	1913	Joins British Red Cross Society, awarded LLA, St. Andrews University, Nephew Richard born.
35	1914	War declared. To Brussels, captured, released to Denmark.
	1915	To Russia, pleurisy, St. George's Medal (Russia), publishes People Who Run.
	1917	Awarded Military Medal and Mons Medal
	1918	To Macedonia. Trains in Textiles, Sweden
40	1919	Brother Denzil dies
	1920	To Egypt (?) Director of Bedouin Industries
	1922	Visits newly discovered tomb of Tutankhamun
	D 1923	Working at Burg el Arab, sees Pavlova dance in Cairo, exhibits Bedouin work in Cairo, Jerusalem & Alexandria, meets Norah Bidulph.
	1924	Nephew John (JP) born
50	1927	To Albania, walks in Pyrenees.
	D 1929	Living in Somerset with Norah Biddulph, visits Ethel Mairet & John Kilbride
	1930	Publishes 'Use of Vegetable Dyes for Beginners'
	D 1931	Exhibiting and selling work, giving weaving and language lessons, attends course in Westerham with Elizabeth Peacock, meets Luther Hooper, tours Finland, T.B. shoulder diagnosed.
	D 1934	Publishes A Short History of Decorative Textiles
	1935	Submits weaving to V&A
	1937	In Almeira, Spanish Civil War
	D 1938	Involved with Womens Territorial Army recruiting campaign
60	1939	War declared, joins WRNS, in Contraband Control
	D 1940	Recruiting & lecturing throughout Britain for Admiralty, meets Duke of Kent
	1941	Intelligence work, Father Dies
	D 1944	Organises craft rooms for WRNS & WAAF in North Wales & Scotland, resigns from WRNS, sister-in-law Christina dies
	D 1945	Catholic Relief Programme, in Italy, Egypt and Austria, private audience with Pope Pius XII,

		made Companion of the Vatican
	D 1946	In Austria with P.O.W.s & displaced persons, in charge of hospital
68	D 1947	Brother Edward Dies, newphew Richard dies
	1951	Living in Cornwall, Mary Mount, Flushing
	1952	Joins Cornwall Guild of Weavers, Spinners &
Dyers		
	1954	Weaves tapestry map of Cornwall
	1956	Publishes Weaving without Tears
	D 1957	President of the Cornwall Guild
	1958	Catholic Womans League, pilgrimage to Rome
80	1959	Article on Bedouin Life in the Egyptian Desert
	D 1960	Weaving & teaching, Peter Collingwood stays at Mary Mount
	D 1964	Publishes Stormy Petrel
	1966	Publishes The Foolish Virgin, advises on crafts in Greece with Dorothy Wilkinson, attends inaugural meeting of the World Crafts Council, British Section.
	D 1968	Visits Spain, Italy, Ireland & Majorca, broadcasts on BBC Weekend Woman's Hour
90	1969	Benidorm
	1970	Sardinia
	1972	Corfu
	1974	Yugoslavia
	1976	Hears Margaret Thatcher speak in St. Austell, advises on Dye Garden at Probus
	1977	Awarded Honorary Life Membership of Cornwall Crafts Association
	1978	April 13, dies in Penryn, Cornwall

D - Pocket diary exists for that year

Source	(Archives) Royal Naval College Greenwich London SE10 9NN	Directorate of Naval Officer App. (S) & WRNS) Ministry of Defence, Ripley Block, Old Admiralty Building
1939	Violetta shown as 1st Officer in the Dec 1939 Naval lists (seniority from 15/11/39)	12/1/39 RC joined for Education duties as 2nd officer WRNS 15/11/39 Seniority to, 1st officer 15/11/1939
1940	Appointed H.M.S. Drake Plymouth	7/6/40 RM Depot Devonport Admin Duties 8/6/40 special duties 6/11/40 – 7/11/40
1941	attached for a short time to H.M.S. Cochrane II (Rosyth HQ) 8/8/41 WRNS HQ	Scottish Travelling Recruiting Officer 7/12/1941 – 14/12/41 Temp Add for WRNS
1942	–/2/42 WRNS OTC Greenwich	15/12/41 Duty at RN College Greenwich – Divisional Instructor Officer to WRNS Officer Training Course
1943		31/1/43 1/2/43 Administrative duties (HMS Pembroke III) outside Admiralty
1944	21/2/44 Appointed Command Education Officer Cochrane –/10/44 does not appear in Naval List after this date.	20/2/44 21/2/44 WRNS Command Education 21/10/44 Officer(HMS Cochrane II) 21/10/44 Released at own request

MEDALS AWARDED TO VIOLETTA THURSTAN

Military Medal
Order of St. George (Russia)
Queen Elizabeth Medal (Belgium)
Mons Star
Allied Medal
Companion of the Vatican
1914 Star with Clasp and roses
British War Medal
Victory Medal

Appendix iii
List of Violetta Thurstan's writings

BOOKS

Field Hospital and Flying Column, G.P. Putnams Sons, London, 1915

The People who Run, G.P. Putnams Sons, 1916

The Use of Vegetable Dyes for Beginners, Dryad Press, 1930

'Plant Dyes in Egypt', series of articles published by Egyptian Horticultural Review (1923), listed as a book in the bibliography of *A Short History of Decorative Textiles* (not seen in this form). Attributed to 1924 in V.T.'s book *The Use of Vegetable Dyes*.

A Short History of Decorative Textiles & Tapestries, Pepler & Sewell, 1934, 2nd edition (1954), 3rd edition (Favil Press, 1972)

Weaving Patterns of Yesterday & Today, Dryad Press (no date, publisher does not know), 3rd edition, Favil Press, London

Weaving without Tears, Museum Press (no date)

Stormy Petrel, self-published from Mary Mount, Flushing, Nr. Falmouth 1964

The Foolish Virgin, Wordens, Marazion (1966)

The Hounds of War Unleashed, United Writers Cornwall, 1978

ARTICLES

in *Quarterly Journal of the Association of the Guild of Weavers, Spinners & Dyers*

'Dyeing in Ancient Times', No. 21, March, 1957

'Plant Dyeing in Ancient Times - Blue Dyes', No. 23, September, 1957

'Dyeing in Ancient Times (Red crimson & scarlet), No. 27, September, 1958

'Bedouin Life in the Libyan Desert' No. 29, March, 1959

'Mortlake 100 Years of Tapestry', No. 79, Autumn 1971

DIARIES in possession of Magdalene College, Cambridge: 1923, 1929, 1931, 1934, 1938, 1944 (x 2), 1945, 1946, 1947, 1952, 1957, 1960, 1964, 1968.

Appendix iv
Examples of diary entries

1923

MARCH 13 TUESDAY

Feria : *purple*.
Birm. : B. Agnellus of Pisa, d.
O.D.C. : S. Euphrasia, v., d., 410.

Trees arrived from the
M. of agriculture - cypress
figs, pomegranates etc.

1923

73—292   WEDNESDAY 14 MARCH

Feria : *purple*.
O.S.A. : B. James of Viterbo ; sd.
O.P. : Octave of S. Thomas Aquinas.

Mr. Dawson invited me
to Pavlova .

? Sollum gets back f. Matruh

Mrs. Dawson & I went
by train to Alex.

I dined with Mr. Dawson
& a small party at the
Union Club & afterwards went
to Pavlova, who was enchanting

Sorrow, borne with resentment and bitterness,
isolates the soul not only from God, but from
her own fellows.—*Mgr. Benson.*

89

Christmas Eve; sd. and d., *purple.*

Arrived Luxor.

Slept Palace Hotel.

Very bright & jolly, lots

of people I knew

Staying in Hotel.

Xmas tree & carols at 6·30

Bay & I visited Luxor Temple

Went to Karnak by moon

light & at 11·30 to midnight —

If any stain or defect had been
the Lord would have sought
Mother for Himself, who shou
free from all sin.—*S. James of*

Mass. 374

CHRISTMAS DAY—THE NATIVITY OF
OUR LORD (Obligation); d1, with Oct,,
white. Three Masses. Cr. Prf. of Nativity
to end of year. Com. of S. Anastasia, v.m.,
304, in Second Mass. Vespers of Festival,
com. S. Stephen, the First Martyr.
Eng.: The Christmas Indulgence begins.

Went to Mass at 9. am.

Afterwards went for a

walk round the town.

Suk today.

Enormous Christmas

Dinner, Lolly afterwards

~~Was a better of whisk~~

That Thou should'st ever bend so low as this!
That Thou should'st ever come so nigh to us so high!
As mortal Babe, should'st feel a Mother's kiss,
And in the compass of a manger lie!
Ah, God! Who art our brother evermore,
It is Thy lowliness that we adore!
—*Q.S.H.*

375

Wednesday 4
(185-180)

8.30. Bishop Matthew. Eden Hotel.

10.0   [illegible]

12.0

Got signal to say Rielle had smashed
herself up in an accident & was in
hospital in Udine. Started off by train
this afternoon - but cannot arrive till
~~particular~~
tomorrow

Thursday 5
(186-179)

Arrived Forli early this morning. Just
missed bus, so got a succession of lifts
(but no breakfast!) first to Ferrara, then
to Padua, and then to Mestre &
finally to Udine.
Went straight to hospital & found Rielle,
not as bad as I had feared - but
with a broken ankle in plaster & her
collar bone fractured. Stayed at
Officers' Transit Hotel

JULY 1945

Friday 6
(187-178)

Went to see Rietler & took Dr Carrulli
to see her. She is going on very well
& I shall be able to leave Tomorrow or
Monday I think

Visited Polish Transit Camp at Udine,
people coming back from slave labour
camps in Germany - most of the
women with small babies, and all in
rags - many of them with vitamin
starvation & other illnesses

Saturday 7
(188-177)

Went with Dr Carrulli to Treviso
to visit the Transit Camps there
Saw Slovene priests 100 of
them who had been there 3 months
& had no books or comforts of any kind
Visited the hospital - no drugs
no dressings - no medical comforts.
Came back very late - but went to
see Rietle who is getting on v. well
leaving tomorrow for Rome

Acknowledgements

For textile connections related to Violetta Thurstan, thanks are due to the Cornwall Guild of Weavers, Spinners and Dyers for the free access to all their Newsletters and scrapbooks. Contributions from Veronica Hudd, Margaret Veale, Britt Varcoe, Alastair Rivers, and W.S. Godfrey have been especially welcome. The Editorial Committee of the Journal for Weavers, Spinners and Dyers have been most encouraging and we thank them for permission to reprint articles and extracts, and to Mary Keer for the use of textile drawings by the late Hilary Chetwynd. Thanks also to Hetty Wickens, Bobbie Cox, Peter Collingwood, Mary Barker, Muriel Harvey, Maggie Giraud (Dartington), Sandra Clark, and the Isle of Wight Guild.

For information on the Catholic connection we are grateful to the Dowager Lady St. Levan, Canon Bede Davis, David Mudd (Radio Cornwall) and Eric Dawkins (Falmouth Town Clerk 1992).

To Robert M. Smart at St. Andrews University, D.J.H. Murphy and Sarah Palmer at Magdalen College, Cambridge, A.P. McGowan (Archivist, Royal Naval College, Greenwich), Veronica Marchbanks (Archives Assistant, British Red Cross), Deborah Burgin (Staff records, Foreign and Commonwealth Office), John Corsellis (Cambridge), Major Johnson (Ministry of Defence), Neil Harvey (Assistant Curator, Textiles & Dress, Victoria & Albert Museum), Margaret Cole (Commander, Directorate of Naval Officers, Ministry of Defence), M.L. Bierbrier (Assistant Keeper, Egyptian Antiquities, British Museum), Celia Petty (Imperial War Museum), Jonathan Evans (Archivist, The Royal London Hospital Trust), Christine Kelly (Royal Geographic Society), Judith Dyer (Bristol Royal Infirmary Library).

For permission to quote extracts, we are grateful to Batsford Publishers, BBC Enterprises, Constable Publishers, David and Charles Publishers, Impact Books, *Guardian* News

Service Ltd., Hodder & Stoughton Publishers, Lemon, Unna & Durbridge, Ltd., Putnam Aeronautical Books, Random House UK, Ltd., Studio Vista Publications, United Writers Publications Ltd., *West Briton* Newspapers, and *The Western Morning News.*

The Librarians at the Penzance and Helston branches of Cornwall County Libraries were most patient and helpful as were the staff at the Slavonic Section of London University, Bristol Royal Infirmary and the Royal Naval Library. To Violetta's family and friends we are deeply indebted. Charles and Margaret Thurstan and their daughter Jill placed all their memorabilia at our disposal, Louise Trubshaw, Anne Pike, Mollie Matthews & Peter Matthewson shared their anecdotes with us.

Early subscribers to this monograph have been much appreciated for their interest and the spur which they gave to our work. These are Ailsa Allaby (Wadebridge), Mrs. D. Atkinson (Ashton), Mrs. Hazel Bowerman (Ladock), Mrs. G. Chamberlain (Truro), Mrs. William Glowacki (Massachusetts), Mrs. J. Martin (St. Austell), Mrs. J. Uren (St. Austell), Miss K.O. Parsons (Chipping Sodbury), J.D. Browne (Warwick), D.S. Dolby (Leamington Spa), Mrs. Ann Howells (Stratford on Avon), Mrs. V. Hudd (Padstow), Mrs. Brit Varcoe (Truro), and G.E. Russ (West Kirby).

Our own friends who collected information, checked references and gave freely of their time deserve special thanks: Tony Trevarthen, Margaret Kyte, Margaret Way, Penny Carter, Philip McMillan Browse, Audrey Pool, Ann Howells, Marjorie Denholm, Mabel Ross, Mary Cox and Sheila Brough. Our sincere thanks to our editor and publisher, Melissa Hardie, of the Jamieson Library, without whom this book would not have been written. Last, not least, we give heartfelt thanks to Kay Smith and Margaret Chinn for sharing their homes with Violetta for longer than they anticipated.

Muriel Somerfield & Ann Bellingham, August 1993

References and Bibliography

Chapter 1 What's in a name

1. Peter Matthewson, in letter to Muriel Somerfield (MS), February, 1992.
2. Quoted from 'A Traveller's Tale' by Sheila Brough, *Cornish Life*, V.3, No. 6, 1976.
3. Foreign & Commonwealth Office from Staff Records Section, in letter to Ann Bellingham (AB), 5 March 1992.
4. Diary entry, 1 February 1929.
5. Quoted from V.T. personal record, as forwarded to Dept. of Geography & History, (Peter Liddle) dated 24.5.77, for the 1914-18 Archive, Sunderland Polytechnic.
6. Family records of Margaret & Charles Thurstan.
7. Ibid.
8. Robert Smart, Keeper of Muniments, University of St. Andrews, in letter to AB, 17 February 1992.
9. Ann Pike, in taped interview of 10 March 1992 followed by letter of 31 March 1992.
10. In letter to Ann Pike from the Canaries, 23 March 1992.
11. V. Thurstan in *Stormy Petrel*, 1964, page 1.
12. Family records of M & C Thurstan, op cit and in letter from Ann Pike to AB, 31 March 1992.
13. Margaret Thurstan in letter to AB, 8 April 1992.

Chapter 2 Education

1. Ann Pike at interview, 10 March 1992.
2. Quoted from *Author's & Writers Who's Who* (1934), Shaw Publishing Company, London and *Author's & Writer's Who's Who* (1963), Burke's Peerage.
3. Jonathan Evans, Librarian, Royal London Hospital Trust (Whitechapel) Archive Centre, in letter to Melissa Hardie, 27 April 1992.
4. Edith Cavell, is the famed English nurse executed by the Germans in Brussels for alleged spying. Further reference in Chapter 3 of this monograph.
5. Royal London Hospital Archives (Whitechapel), *op cit*, Note 3.
6. *Ibid.*

7. Letter from V. Marchbanks, Archives Assistant, British Red Cross, with map of Macedonia, 25 March 1992.

8. University of St. Andrews Archives, *op cit*, Chapter 1, Note 8.

9. *Ibid.*

10. Quoted from a personal letter to Marjory Denholm from anon. friend, 12 January 1993. Copied to A.B. on 22 January 1993.

Chapter 3 'War, war, war'

1. Quoted from John Elliot, *The Fall of Eagles*, BBC Publications, 1974.

2. V. Thurstan in *Field Hospital and Flying Column*, Being the Journal of an English Nursing Sister in Belgium & Russia, G.P. Putnam's Sons, 1915.

3. V. Thurstan in *Hounds of War Unleashed*, A Nurse's Account of her Life on the Eastern Front during the 1914-18 War, United Writers, Cornwall, 1978.

4. *Ibid.*

5. *Ibid.*

6. 'One Woman's War 1914-1918, February 1985, parish newsletter, Falmouth, referring to VT.

7. Farmborough, F. *Nurse at the Russian Front: A Diary 1914-18*, Constable, London, 1974.

8. V. Thurstan in *The People Who Run*, Being the Tragedy of the Refugees in Russia, G.P. Putnam's Sons, 1916.

9. Ibid., p. 1

10. Quoted from *West Briton & Royal Cornwall Gazette*, Thursday, 27 April 1978.

11. Britt Varcoe in letter to MS, February 1993.

Chapter 4 Beginning to weave

1. *Op. cit*, Chapter 1, Note 5.

2. From original letter of Denzil Thurstan to V.T., family records, 15 October 1912.

3. V. Thurstan, *Weaving Without Tears*, Museum Press, London 1956.

4. V. Thurstan, *A Short History of Decorative Textiles*, Peplar & Sewall, London, 1934.

5. Anecdote from W.S. Godfrey, member of the Cornwall Guild, 1992.

6.'Warp and Weft', London Guild of Weavers, No. 62, June, 1966.

7. L. Brown and S. Rachid, *Egyptian Carpets*, American University in Cairo Press, 1985.

8. Peter Collingwood in letter to MS, 7 February 1992.

9. Diary entry, Friday, 22 June 1923.

10. K. Grasset (London School of Weaving) is the author of *The Complete Guide to Hand Spinning,* and other weaving books.

11. Obituary of VT, *Op cit*, Chapter 3, Note 10.

12. Confirmed by the British Museum, Dept. of Egyptian Antiquities in letter of M.L. Bierbrier to AB, 31 March 1992.

13. S. Brough, *Op cit*, Chapter 1, Note 2.

14. Certificate of Candidate for Election, FRGS, Royal Geographical Society, 19 May 1924.

15. H. Fox, *Woven from a Stone,* The Story of the Quantock Weavers, 1974.

16. V. Thurstan, *Use of Vegetable Dyes for Beginners,* Dryad Press, 1930, 15th edition, 1977, three reprints since.

17. See M. Coatts, *A Weaver's Life: Ethel Mairet, 1872-1952,* Crafts Council, 1983. Also Stuart Robinson, *A Fertile Field,* 1983, Guild of Gloucester Craftsmen & Cheltenham Art Gallery.

Chapter 5 Living & Weaving

1. Diary entry, 15 April 1931.

2. Diary entries, 1931

3. Hilda Breed, sometime lecturer at Avery Hill College, Eltham, London. Weaver and teacher of weaving and member of the Crafts Centre of Great Britain.

4. 'Dorothy Wilkinson', article in *Quarterly Journal of Guilds,* No. 63, September, 1967.

5. Alice Hindson, sometime lecturer, Central School of Art, specialised in draw loom weaving.

6. H. Fox, *Op cit*, Chapter 4, Note 15.

7. V. Thurstan, *Op cit, A History of Decorative Textiles,* Foreword.

8. Bobbie Cox in letter to MS of 9 December 1991.
9. Diary entry, Sunday, 3 June 1934.
10. *Op cit*, Chapter 4, Note 3.

Chapter 6 And more war
1. A.P. McGowan, Archivist, Royal Naval College, Greenwich, in letter to AB, 4 March 1992.
2. Ann Pike in letter to AB, 31 March 1992.
3. Diary entry, 10 January 1938. Despite this entry, subsequent reprints have been issued by Favil Press.
4. Diary entry, 11 March 1938.
5. Ministry of Defence in letter to AB, 20 February 1992.
6. Cmdr. M. Cole, WRNS by letter, 31 March 1992.
7. *Op cit*, Note 1.
8. Vera Laughton Mathews in *Blue Tapestry*, Hollis & Carter, 1949, p. 98.
9. Mary Barker in letter to MS, 9 September 1991.
10. Diary entry, 14 October 1944.

Chapter 7 Gathering loose ends
1. Diary entry, Saturday, 20 January 1945.
2. Sunderland Polytechnic, *op cit*, Chapter 1, Note 5.

Chapter 8 Tieing the knots
1. Foreign & Commonwealth Office, *op cit*, Chapter 1, Note 3.
2. Sunderland Polytechnic, *op cit*, Chapter 1, Note 5.
3. John Corsellis is a retired solicitor residing in Cambridge, compiler of the Nuffield Foundation book on the two waves of Yugoslavian refugees.
4. Letters from V. Thurstan courtesy of J. Corsellis.
5. V. Thurstan, *The Foolish Virgin*, Wordens, Marazion, 1966.

Chapter 9 Cornwall
1. Peter Matthewson, *op cit*, Chapter 1, Note 1.
2. *Ibid.*
3. Leonard and Dorothy Elmhirst were the Founder Trustees of the Dartington Hall enterprise near Totnes, Devon.
4. R. Tanner, *Double Harness*, Impact Books, London.

5. 'Peasant Art in Norway' by VT in *Cornwall Guild News-letter*, No. 7, December 1954.

6. Muriel Harvey to MS, November, 1991.

7. 'A Note on Teazles', *Cornwall Guild Newsletter*, No. 10, 1956.

8. Peter Collingwood, OBE, abandoned medicine to become a full-time weaver 40 years ago, concentrating on rugs and wall-hangings. He has written three definitive works on textiles.

9. V. Thurstan, 'Dyeing in Ancient Times' in *Quarterly Journal of the Guilds*, No. 21, March 1957.

10. V. Thurstan, 'Plant Dyeing in Ancient Times - Blue Dyes', *Journal of Guilds*, No. 23, September 1957.

11. V. Thurstan, 'Dyeing in Ancient Times - Red, Crimson & Scarlet Dyes', *Journal of Guilds, No. 27, September 1958.*

12. Mary Barker, *op cit*, Chapter 6, Note 8.

13. Mollie Matthews and Canon A. Bede Davis, in conversation with MS and AB, 8 March 1992.

14. Extract from *Cornwall Guild Newsletter*, No. 49, January 1966.

15. Extract from *Cornwall Guild Newsletter*, No. 52, September 1966.

16. Hilda Breed in *Quarterly Journal of the Guilds*, No. 63, September 1967.

17. Extract from *Cornwall Guild Newsletter*, No. 53, January 1967.

18. Ibid.

19. Extract from *Cornwall Guild Newsletter*, No. 54, April 1967.

20. Extract from *Cornwall Guild Newsletter*, No. 57, January 1968.

Chapter 10 'her indomitable spirit'

1. *Cornwall Guild Newsletter*, No. 61, December 1968.

2. Margery Hicks in *Cornwall Guild Newsletter*, No. 63, April 1969.

3. *Cornwall Guild Newsletter*, No. 68, January 1971.

4. V. Thurstan, 'Mortlake: 100 Years of Tapestry', *Quarterly Journal of the Guilds*, No. 79, Autumn, 1971.

5. Hetty Wickens in letter to MS, 2 September 1991.

6. *Cornwall Guild Newsletter*, No. 80, March 1974.
7. *Cornwall Guild Newsletter*, No. 81, June 1974
8. *Cornwall Guild Newsletter*, No. 83, January 1974.
9. *Cornwall Guild Newsletter*, No. 87, January 1976.
10. A series of programmes, the first of which was broadcast on September 7, 1976. Reported in *Cornwall Guild Newsletter*, No. 90, August 1976.
11. S. Brough, *op cit*, Chapter 1, Note 2.
12. B. Wall in *The Packet*, 29 April 1977.
13. V. Thurstan, *op cit*, Chapter 3, Note 3.
14. Margery Hicks became a professional weaver, served six years in WRAF in WWII, and contributed articles to *Cornish Review*, *Countryman*, *The Lady* and *The Journal of the Association of Guilds*. Newsletter No. 94, April 1978 for this obituary.
15. Initials following the anecdotes refer to the following people:
MB Mary Barker, SB Sheila Brough, WSG W. S. Godfrey, MM Mollie Matthews, AP Ann Pike, DLSL The Dowager Lady St. Levan, CT Charles Thurstan, MT Margaret Thurstan, VT Violetta Thurstan, LT Louise Trubshaw, MV Margaret Veale.

* * * * *

Further reading, in addition to books and articles mentioned in references.

Brittain, V. (1933) *Testament of Youth*, Fontana.
Caldecott, L. (1984) *Women of our Century*, Ariel Books .
Collingwood, Peter (1968) *Techniques of Rug Weaving*, Faber & Faber.
Hooper, L. (1910) *Handloom Weaving, Plain & Ornamental*, John Hogg.
Robinson, J. (1990) *Wayward Women*, A guide to women travellers, OUP
Robinson, S. (1969) *A History of Dyed Textiles*, Studio Vista.
         (1983) *A Fertile Field*, Guild of Gloucestershire Craftsmen & Cheltenham Art Gallery & Museum.
Wickens, H. (1983) *Natural Dyes for Spinners & Weavers*, Batsford.

INDEX

Sutton, Ann 63,66
Sweden 19-20,29,35
Tanner, Robin, 58
Textiles 58,62-3
Thurstan, family: Tree 6, Charles 3,5,57,76,& wife Margaret 5,78, Denzil (bro) 5,19,Edward Paget 4,23,34,35,43,53,57,62 & wife Christina 4,34,43, John Denzil (JP) 5,53,57-8,74,78,(Aunt) Louise 4,34,Norman 5, Richard 5,57.
Thurstan, Violetta, Age discrepancies 1-2,51, birth 1-2, catholicism (see Catholicism, Roman) 57-8,character 1-2,7,10,42,48-9,52 Cornish roots 1,3-4,6, in Cornwall 57ff, Cornwall Guild President 59ff, death 2,74-5, education 4,7-10, health 29,32-3,49, letters to J. Corsellis 54-6,life membership CCA 73, Matron of Marcelline (Belgium) 13-4, Medals 16,17-8,47,74,Append ii, Mother 3-4, name change 1, nursing/hospital experiences 8-9, 12ff, Places of residence (see list at end of this index), pottery 36, in Spain 37-8, teaching 2,59,71, writings 2-3, see list Append iii.
Times, The 2
Treviso Camp 47
Tripoli 46
Trubshaw, Louise 77-8
Tscherning, Madam 15
Tut-ankh-Amun 25
UNRRA 44,46,53
Urchefort Manor (Wilts) 71
Use of Vegetable Dyes for Beginners Fore, 26-7
VADs 12
Varcoe, Britt 72,73
Victoria & Albert Museum 35,58,66,71
Volkonsky, Prince & Princess 15
Wales 42
Wall, Brian 74
Way, Margaret 36
Weaving Without Tears 18,35,59
Western Morning News 61
Wickens, Hetty 68(photo),71
Wilkinson, Dorothy 32,38,40,60,65,69

113

Known places of residence: Violetta Thurstan *

a. Canaries: Casa Marina, Tenereife
b. Apple Tree Cottage, Kingston, Taunton
c. Tredegar House, Bow
d. Dragon House, Washford, near Minehead
e. Hopscott, near Minehead
f. Dragon House, Bookay Down, Kingswear, South Devon
g. South Avenue, Corsham (Bath Academy)
h. Mary Mount, Flushing, nr. Falmouth, Cornwall
i. Old Mill House, Penryn, nr. Falmouth, Cornwall

*This is an incomplete record. Ed.